LEAVING
LUCIFER

Part I
THE BEGINNING

What Eve began Mary doth end...Arcane legend

ELIZABETH ROMIG

BALBOA.
PRESS
A DIVISION OF HAY HOUSE

Balboa Press books may be ordered through booksellers or by contacting:

Balboa Press
A Division of Hay House
1663 Liberty Drive
Bloomington, IN 47403
www.balboapress.com
1 (877) 407-4847

Because of the dynamic nature of the Internet, any web addresses or links contained in this book may have changed since publication and may no longer be valid. The views expressed in this work are solely those of the author and do not necessarily reflect the views of the publisher, and the publisher hereby disclaims any responsibility for them.

The author of this book does not dispense medical advice or prescribe the use of any technique as a form of treatment for physical, emotional, or medical problems without the advice of a physician, either directly or indirectly. The intent of the author is only to offer information of a general nature to help you in your quest for emotional and spiritual well-being. In the event you use any of the information in this book for yourself, which is your constitutional right, the author and the publisher assume no responsibility for your actions.

Any people depicted in stock imagery provided by Thinkstock are models, and such images are being used for illustrative purposes only. Certain stock imagery © Thinkstock.

Print information available on the last page.

ISBN: 978-1-5043-4910-9 (sc)
ISBN: 978-1-5043-4912-3 (hc)
ISBN: 978-1-5043-4911-6 (e)

Library of Congress Control Number: 2016900579

Balboa Press rev. date: 02/15/2016

This book is dedicated to Cindy, who reminded me and to my children Eppie, Mattie, James and Peter.

PREFACE

When I first told my son, James that I had finally finished this book he asked me what the title would be.

I told him, "*Leaving Lucifer/Part One: The Beginning*"

"Oh no, mom. You're trip to India seemed so light and fun. Why that name, it sounds so dark?"

"Yes, I know but that is why the title includes, Part One*: The Beginning*. I put that in there to separate the India experience from the more serious aspects of my long journey and experiments with Truth. *Leaving Lucifer; The End* isn't included."

With that said, he approved of my title and I hope you will understand; this is meant to be a fun story.

So, picture, if you will, the hippie days -- those great days where the likes of *hey man, far out* and *bummer* commingled with the likes of Om, Shakti, Nirvana and Kama Sutra. What a mix! This was in 1974 and I had just turned 24 when I began my non-mainstream adventure to India. People were everywhere and searching for everything.

This is not a scholarly work. I have made every effort to preserve the writing in the naiveté of my youth as seen through the eyes of the soul. This straightforward story will show you how a small degree of simple-minded, dumb-luck wanderlust can set the compass to higher altitudes where the air is thin and only the heart can travel.

Special thanks to Bhante, the beloved Buddhist monk who taught me. I also give thanks for the precious souls that survived the journey with me and provided countless opportunities for me to learn life lessons, which have taken me further down the path than I ever thought possible.

"We can argue 'till we are all blue in the face but the bottom line is this; we see everything upside down and backward and there is nothing your brain can do to stop that. The brain actually performs a great function in doing this. It levels the playing field when people begin to realize this because that is when we can begin the journey. This Work is in the heart."

I thought a moment about what he had just said. I knew this was a scientific fact yet, had never given it much thought. My mind raced; seeking out that tiny space where we might not be controlled by this optical illusion. I could not grasp it; I could not outthink the thought…

"This world we see, being upside down and backward, is the Luciferian World. It has its purpose but we must all leave it eventually." The Teacher

CHAPTER 1

I had just finished my shift and was settling down to get some much-needed sleep in the back of our Mercedes van where the single-sized mattresses were stacked two wide and four deep. I could not tell you where we were. It could have been Turkey, Iran or Afghanistan. Everyone else was sleeping soundly; all neatly tucked in to their personal bed rolls, much like a tin of King Oscar sardines. That is with the exception of the driver, Adam, William and I.

"What a great picture that would make." I told Adam.

I was looking at William as he worked on the electrical wiring for the backdoor lighting. Other than the small bulb that William was working on, there was no light in the van or outside in the middle of nowhere; no street lights, no headlights, no homes - nothing. We were rocking back and forth as we navigated the many twist and turns of the mountain highway. The light bulb shifted as William worked the wires causing golden sprays of light to shower over him. In spite of the motion, William was on his knees and leaning into the task remaining focused and intent on his project. His thin nimble fingers tugged at the wiring.

As I watched William, I thought of the Scarecrow from *the Wizard of Oz*. His flaxen hair, which was thin and straight, hung down in strands beneath his fedora. His slender face had shadows moving across it; back and forth in unison with the van's movement.

"Take a mental picture and you will have it forever" replied Adam.

Snap. Picture taken, I fell asleep ...

CHAPTER 2

Googling *1974 maps of Euro/Asia*, a colorful plot of countries with cities and veins of roadways popped up on the screen. Reaching up with my index finger I slowly followed along the route we had taken; France, Switzerland, Austria, Bulgaria, Yugoslavia, Turkey, Iran, Afghanistan, Pakistan, **India**. It hurt a little to look at the route and realize that even if I wanted to return via the same roadways, it was now impossible. Yugoslavia no longer exists, along with civil unrest and war in other countries, the long trek is a hazard at best.

It was in the sunset days of the Counter-Cultural Revolution or hippie days as I knew them, when I set out on my mystical journey bound for India for the purpose of studying under a Venerable Cambodian Buddhist Monk. We called him Bhante (translation-*monk*). He was in his eighties at that time. Bhante had founded the Ashoka Mission in 1948 when he was given a 12 acre tract of land on the outskirts of Delhi, India. He was a Master of Vipassana/Color Meditation and a well-known healer. He was a Theravada Buddhist; "The way of the Elders". A discipline that they consider most closely follows the original teachings and practices of the Buddha. This was his one and only course of study that he offered to the world. I was fortunate to be one of his few students. Bhante died in 1999 at the tender age of 110.

It's hard to say when this all started for me; or to figure out where it all begins. The beginning perhaps takes place at my birth and then I ask what birth is and what death is. Is there any beginning or end? I cannot remember a time that I didn't ponder things like this; constantly obsessing over the slightest issue. Do our pets go to heaven; does an ant know I am up here looking down at it? So, forget about it; I will just start. I am a person that never followed merrily down someone else's path and I always, had to test and question everything. I can see clearly now that although I am not a scientist I do have a certain scientific expectation of the unknown.

There are many influences that shape our lives aren't there? I can think of two influences that caused me to wiggle my way "out of the box". A major contributor to my future life was Mrs. Parsons, our nanny. I don't know when she showed up but I was probably no more than four when she came. She was a widow and her husband had been a minister. By the time I was four years old there were five of us and one more was on the way. My mother needed the help; in all she had 11 children.

Mrs. Parsons would brush and braid my hair and talk to me while I sat there fidgeting and anxious; rolling my eyes. She told me two things that I did not like. First – "You are a worry wart, you worry about everything." Second, "You are just like that poem, *"There was a little girl, who had a little curl, right in the middle of her forehead and when she was good, she was quite good but when she was bad, she was horrid"*." I cringed at these remarks. I had a volatile temper and did indeed worry about everything. She was correct in her observations. I don't want you to think that she said this with unkindness. In looking back, I can say she was dispassionate in her critiques. In turn it caused me to view these traits in a straightforward manner. At four years old, I was painfully self-aware.

Mrs. Parsons' help in observation and my melancholy nature had led me to lead a life of prayer and contemplation. Those are high minded words that can only be used now at age sixty because if you had asked me at any point in those growing years if I was prayerful or contemplative, I would have trembled and felt I had committed a grievous sin. Perhaps I was too aware for my own good yet I remain grateful to Mrs. Parsons' insightful talks with me and I am grateful to God for forming me in my mother's womb; creating me in forever.

Fast forward to 1973, nineteen years later, when a second life altering event occurred in that I embraced the concept of the Kingdom of God; the impression of which created a yearning in me that would never be satisfied with mundane disciplines...

CHAPTER 3

I was born in December of 1949 in Anchorage, Alaska. What a beautiful land; full of mountains with year-round cold fresh-water streams, fields of colorful wildflowers, animals; moose, sheep, bears, all kinds of wild things, roaming-perhaps high on the mountain cliffs or in the wood outside your home and lastly, air that was fresh, clean and cold. The sun never set in the summer, contrasting the dark, cold winters where the sun never seemed to be anything but a distant star that left no shadows. Yet, even this does not express in full the experience of being born and raised in Alaska. What a tremendous time and place it was back then. The land; The Great Land, emanates a strong force which can turn on a dime; step out of line and there is a severe price to pay for stupidity. Many tragic accidents attest to this; those untamed freedoms keep Alaskans in Alaska regardless of the price one pays for carelessness.

It was a beautiful time of life for me and what kept me so nurtured was not my parents but this sense of nurturing energy coming from the earth itself. I believe it was a significant influence in an otherwise gloomy childhood. This all added up to a person that sought solutions and resolved not to live the life her parents chose. Alaska had its beauty but I had to venture out and make my own discoveries.

Before the pipeline days of the late 60's and beyond Alaska was a different place. We resembled more of a universal culture. Alaska was an international stopover, before jumbo jets and improved airways made traveling over the pole outdated. It still is a melting pot but not like then. It was not unusual to walk down the street and hear another language being spoken or see "foreigners" dressed in their European styles. There was a pioneer spirit on the streets; everyone that came to Alaska to live in the early days had rejected or been rejected from the conformity of the *lower 48* society. Many others came from other parts of the world for pretty much the same reasons. The door to our house on the corner of 5th and L Street was never locked. It is now a bed and breakfast.

After the discovery of oil in Prudhoe Bay and when the boom hit, a different kind of energy blew into the Alaskan ether. I noticed this in the early 70's. We still had our pioneer spirit but I sensed a shift in the wind back then. Something innocent was being taken away. The influx of people, the crime, and materialism all contributed to a thinning of our natural heartiness. I don't mean that Alaska hadn't seen boom and bust in days before; where some real characters came seeking their fortune in gold, earlier oil fields and all the other trappings (literal or otherwise) that go along with boom or bust economies, but this was a change that I personally experienced. Once, while talking with an old pioneer, he pointed to the change that came when oil was discovered on the Kenai Peninsula. That was before I could remember. Another would probably go back further to the Gold Rush. Then we have the Russians and the world explorers like Captain Cook. It goes on and on; the Alaskan Natives have endured it all and remain the truest residents of the Great Land; my family was a pioneering family.

Family history can make us proud but most of all it should keep us humble. There is always something good and always something bad discovered in the genealogy. In the end we are all really on our own and accountability becomes personal. My kin in Alaskan history began in the late 1800's when my grandfather came to Alaska as a missionary and a doctor. My father was born in Seward, Alaska; then there are all of his offspring (or a goodly portion), being born Alaska. That is where I begin. My mom haled from Wisconsin; she and my dad met in Adak, Alaska during World War II.

I recount the Alaskan summers which were always wild and fun for me. We had a few summer cabins where we spent our entire summer break from school. We would leave the city soon after the last day of the school year to take off for the main cabin in Cooper Landing. My father stayed behind, maintaining his medical practice; flying down in his Cessna 180 on the weekends. Cooper Landing is one hundred miles south of Anchorage on the Kenai Peninsula. It is a small "pass through" on your way to the larger towns like Soldotna, Kenai or Homer and is situated on Kenai Lake. Kenai Lake is a glacier fed lake which explains its milky green color. The water from melting glaciers carries lots of silt with it which creates this sea green milk-glass appearance. The local population has always fluctuated but when I was young a lot of us were summer residents. My family would stay for the beginning of the school year in Cooper Landing so that the small community would have a large enough headcount to warrant a teacher for the tiny one-room school house. Once the water froze in the pipes, we headed back to the city to finish the school year. My mom always remarked that we were ahead of the city schools whenever we transferred back into them.

During the summer in Cooper Landing, we would walk the mountain paths to get as high up as possible; just skirting the timberline where the forest ended and the rocky top-half of the mountains began. My brothers would go even farther; way up to the rocky cliffs. I have done that only once in my life but what an adventure. I was with my younger brother Ben. We saw hoary marmots popping up right at the edge of the tree line in the grassy fields and mountain goats on the rocky cliffs. We tried like crazy to sneak up on the mountain goats but they kept going higher to loftier rocky cliffs. Seeing the futility in mountain goat chasing, we sat down to rest; drinking our warm beer and eating our lunch of Tillamook cheese and salami on pilot bread. At this height, we could see just the red roofing of the main cabin of our summer home. I sat and watched as the leaves of distant trees far below us changed colors as the wind swept through branches of quaking aspen, cottonwood and birch while the scrub pine leaned this way and that. The cars on the highway beneath us appeared as miniatures. Every now and then, a rear view mirror would catch the sun and send out a sharp reflection.

When we finally descended from the high viewpoint to the highway below, there was Lana Spielman and her friend waiting to greet us. She was a good friend of my sister Ella's. Lana and her friend were taking a drive from Anchorage and had stopped to watch *the climbers* (us). We were all surprised to see each other and laughed and talked for a little while. They went on their way down to Kenai and we headed for the cabin, which was across the lake on Snug Harbor Road. It was a beautiful sunny summer day when we did this and it remains one of my fondest memories of Cooper Landing.

Here, in Cooper Landing, we spent endless days on Kenai Lake, rowing and rowing, crossing over to Millie's Kenai Lake Lodge to eat freshly made French fried potatoes and drink cans of cold Coke. It was endless adventure for us. In the nighttime, if the lake was calm, we took the boat and rowed far out of our little cove to see other summer homes and to see who might have come down for the weekend. This was often late so we did not go to shore to visit anyone but made notes to go checking up the next day.

We traveled like a pack of wild animals. Never enough life vests in the boat and no gun on the short walks up the mountain paths. No one ever drowned or was mauled so it's not worth worrying about now. Quite literally, once you learned to walk and talk a little, you were grabbed by the family pack and participated in all the shenanigans. I can still see my baby brother Karl in a diaper sitting on one of the seats of our Boston Whaler -- no life vest that I can recall. We had them in the boat but weren't consistent in wearing them and I am almost sure we didn't have enough to save us all if necessary.

There were movies held at the community club, which was a large one-story, two-room log structure. They were movies like *Black Scorpion* or *Godzilla*; all B type movies. An old pioneer by the name of Andy Anderson, who reminded me of Albert Schweitzer, was responsible for picking the movies and I don't know if he liked these movies or was just too cheap to pick out good ones. During the weekday, my mother would make the drive to the post office, which was housed in a private dwelling. After the post office and heading home, she would pull over to the corrugated metal garage in front of the community club to see if Andy had pasted the latest movie poster to its wall. We didn't care what was showing. The movie provided a place for the locals to get together and if we were fortunate, we would stop off at the local store before the movie to pay hugely inflated prices for candy bars and cans of soda.

Our Upper Russian compound was up around the mountains from Cooper Landing and on the Upper Russian Lake. Unlike the milky green of Kenai Lake, Upper Russian Lake is a clear-water lake. We would spend a few days to a week here and there at Upper Russian throughout the summer and our Juneau Lake cabin was used mainly for the fall hunting season. I personally spent even less time at Juneau Lake.

Upper Russian Lake was my favorite summer home. It always struck me as an ancient ruin of some kind -- the primordial essence of man's first steps as man. Most people that have visited Upper Russian will say the same. It has a strong mystical pulse that seems to whisper the past. There is no other private land on the lake; the rest of the 3,000 acres surrounding our cabin is all part of the Andy Simon Wildlife Refuge. We had forty acres with bragging rights to the only sandy beach on the entire lake. Our property was on one end of the lake with our beach being shaped like a crescent moon that embraced the cove; our cove.

To get to Upper Russian Lake, we either hiked the nine mile trail from Cooper Landing or arranged a flight in with the local bush pilot in Cooper Landing or Moose Pass. There in that beautiful cabin, built by homesteaders Luke and Mamie Elwell we spent hours playing pinochle on the long kitchen table or reading from the seemingly endless supply of old magazines and yellowed paper-back books they had left behind. I discovered many classics in that cabin. The cabin was built on a small hill. It was a long cabin with windows that rendered a spectacular view to Upper Russian Lake. From the kitchen windows one could see the far end of the two mile lake and the mountains beyond.

You could watch the weather patterns change up at the other end of the lake in the high mountain passes. "It goes all the way to Seward; those clouds forming up there will get to Seward if the wind is right or it will come our way and we can expect rain in a few hours." my father would tell us.

By watching the clouds moving in or out he could guess what the weather was in Seward. He would sit there with us looking out to the far end and watch as storms came in or moved on. We could hear the waves from the cabin in gentle swish sweepings on clear sunny days to fierce lathery thrashings during the stormy ones.

Along with the National Geographic magazines and paperbacks, the former owners had also left behind all kinds of hand crafted things such as tables, chairs, towel racks, things like ashtrays made from tin cans, etc. One item that I just loved was a weather vane. It was a small wooden propeller attached to a piece of wood that was anchored into the ground. It was right outside the bunk area of the main cabin so that when the rain and winds came the propeller would start a whirring; turning wildly to and fro as the waves rendered a severe beating to the shoreline. It was comforting to wake up hearing all of this. It meant a warm fire and a long day of reading or cooking. There was never a bad day at Upper Russian; rain or shine.

As I grew into my teen years, I would have the caretaker, Bill Morrison, gas up the kicker and I would take our small boat putt-putting around the two mile lake; going in and out of the many coves. I traveled slowly around the lake; heading out of our cove and turning right. Each cove had its own personality. Along this side of the lake to the right and going around, there was little to no shoreline. Bill told the story of how he had taken a long string of line with him in the boat and tossed it over the side to measure the depth. "I had what I figured at least 50 foot of rope dropped over and it never touched the bottom." It was deep over there and its sudden plunge into the unknown cast an ominous shadow over my adventure. I scurried past this part heading for the more gentle shorelines.

A little further along, there were some nice little coves with modest beaches where I'd shut the engine off to listen for sounds of nature. I never landed on shore in the coves. I cut the engine and went parallel to the shore some twenty or so feet out. I was safe from anything that might show up on the shore line but assured a view of whatever might appear.

Trees would groan and sway and leaves would rustle. Occasionally, I would hear an unknown animal tearing through the forest. Sometimes it would indicate a large animal such as a moose or bear with the loud snapping and crashing of alder branches, or sometimes it might have been a rabbit or other small creature; padded feet softly scampering away. Each cove had its own unique characteristic, which I grew to recognize.

Further on and across the lake from our cabin, the Russian River spills into Upper Russian Lake. This area had a stronger sense of ruggedness. I could look into the wilderness following the river's path as it disappeared into the tangled mass of green alders. The mountains that followed the river into Seward were sharp like dragons teeth. Up there - on one of those mountains was a waterfall and every time I came to this spot, I would cut the engine and listen attentively and with intent. I swore I heard the water tumbling over those distant and jagged cliffs.

One day, my brother, Howard and I boated over to that area. Cutting the engine, we looked down into the crystal clear water. Beneath us were layers of fish swimming between, around and above one another. I have no idea how deep the water was but it was almost dizzying to stare down into the depths and see the many levels. There were some of the largest trout I had ever seen moving about the spawning salmon. Howard tried like crazy to hook just one but they were too full of roe to cast a glance at the baited hook. It was frustrating to see the hook plummet down and hang there-suspended in the clear water with the most tempting bait and the fish not giving a darn.

I easily lost track of time as I went in and out of the lake's many indents. At a certain point, I would see the high mountains become shadowed; letting me know it was time to get back and

I'd speed up and head toward home. It got to be a challenge for me to rev up the engine, make a sharp left turn in to our cove and then cut the engine at just the right moment to gently glide to shore feeling light as a feather.

I would tie off the boat to an old gray tree stump that protruded out of the small hillside and walk slowly up the path to the cabin. The warmth of the kitchen would greet me as I entered. There was always a fire in the stove and a kettle of hot water mildly steaming on the stoves surface. I would fix a cup of tea and watch the mountains darken. I could see the daylight far off but the tall mountains provided shading as the earth slowly moved through time. Dark never really came in the summer.

Our Juneau Lake cabin was a small hike from Cooper Landing or a short flight by charter. It was an old Trapper's Cabin. A Trapper's Cabin was a standard design in Alaska built by the old timers for their winters on the trap line. It is a one room log structure and usually has a sod roof. It is dark inside, windows mean heat loss; there might be a few but the eaves hang over to the extent that nothing directly shines into the cabin. There were bunk beds in the back and the rest of the room had a kitchen table and chairs, wood stove and built in shelves along the front walls by the door.

For two weeks, my dad and brothers (some sisters) would go to the Juneau lake cabin for fall moose hunting and if they were fortunate, they managed to bag enough moose to last our large family a whole year. The meat would be skinned and quartered and heavily peppered at Juneau Lake and flown out to Cooper Landing; it would then be hung in the meat house for curing up. After it had hung long enough, my dad would butcher the quarters.

My father, being a doctor, would cut the meat like a professional butcher. Rump roast, hunter (round) steaks, sirloin, brisket, etc., were wrapped and marked and put in the freezer. Back then I ate my share of meat and loved the rich organic taste of moose meat. We all learned to cook moose meat and we were all good cooks.

Our Cooper Landing home had all the amenities; electricity, running water, indoor toilet and bath. The other two cabins were strictly rustic; we cooked on the wood stove, hauled our water from the nearby streams or lakes and used an outhouse. I preferred the rustic way of life. Hauling water and outhouse facilities was the price to pay for having solitude and living close to nature. It could get lonesome at times at our Upper Russian cabin and often one of my sibs would say, "Be quiet, I think I hear a plane coming." We would stop what we were doing to listen, hoping it would be someone flying in to pay a visit. Nine times out of ten it was wishful thinking and we would all return to our reading or card playing keeping our ears tuned in to the sounds, hoping for company.

I say "we" throughout my childhood memories because as I said before, my brothers and sisters, all of us, relied on each other for playmates. We were close back then. We were always up to one thing or another; climbing in or out of windows, sledding down the hill in our back yard, building snow forts, throwing snowballs at the cars that passed by. You name it; we did it.

After one of my siblings fell from one of the second-story windows, my dad had netting attached to each window so that we would be caught if we fell out. I have seen a few black and white photos that show the heavy nets around our windows and when I see those old pioneer pictures it brings back a flood of memories.

We could laugh and play and then there's this other big thing called alcoholism and the sad and frightening times that I, as a child was exposed to.

As a result of the chaos that took place at home, I began my life of prayer when I was a young girl. Many times I could be overwhelmed with fear, and praying brought peace. I experienced that force entering my room and taking away my fears and helping me to fall to sleep. Through these efforts and experience, I didn't question if God existed. I don't want to preach here; this is how it worked for me and it is important to honor everyone's ideal of a Creator or not. I am grateful for my answered prayers. It became part of my daily existence; prayer was part of everything I did. As I have said, I was a constant thinker and worry wart and prayer or generally talking to God about everything was just part of my nature. Without fail a solution would come. I leaned on this and frankly I believe God got a little sick of me. I don't blame Him; I could be an awful whiner.

In retrospect, I am able to see that the gift of Discernment was awake in me from as far back as I can remember. I was able to see people from an inner vantage point; without making distinctions and I had no ability to shut it down. If things troubled me, I would consider the nature of the problem, reviewing it in as much detail a child could give. In the process answers would come. For instance, there was a time when I was nine years old that I became aware of capital punishment. A girl had just moved into our neighborhood from outside (*the lower 48*). She was mature for being ten years old and she told me about all kinds of world events that up until then I had never heard. One story she related to me was the story of a man that had killed someone and how after they caught him he was executed in the electric chair.

The information disturbed me to the point that when I returned to my house, I went to my bedroom to mull over the situation. I thought about executions and wondered if I thought it was right. Out of blue it came to me, clear and precise, the death penalty was wrong. I shuddered at the thought of such criminals, but in the end I understood the death penalty was not the solution. Then I worried about Alaska; did we have the death penalty? I went to my mother and asked her about the death penalty; she assured me that we didn't have it. I was so relieved to know that Alaskans weren't killing people. I honestly don't know what I would have done if we were living in a place that used the death penalty. It was a deep insight that lacked the restrictions I might otherwise have self-imposed.

Such illuminations in childhood developed my contemplative and prayerful nature to such a degree that all other things were less significant. I maintained a firm opponent of the death penalty from that day forward.

CHAPTER 4

By the time I turned 23, I had become an idealistic and passionate young woman without a care in the world. I graduated from high school but wanted no part of college with what I had come to term, "canned intelligence". From my perspective I found most education a form of copying and not learning.

It was the hippie days and I fully embraced the counter culture. I believed in an end to wars, racism and gross materialism. As a contemplative I had formed definite opinions and ideals by this time. Like many during that time period, I seemed to be growing from the inside out; I never questioned if God existed. But then there was also the external person that had the normal day to day struggles of just plain living. I always saw these two aspects as separate parts of me stitched together with words and personality.

The days of free thinking and the non-mainstream life style appealed immensely to me. It was natural to gravitate to hippie ideals without thinking "oh, I'm a hippie", especially for an Alaskan. Churches did not interest me; I saw them as controlling; an extension of "Big Brother". Although I felt close to spirituality in general, I never experienced such closeness in religious organizations.

My immediate group of friends discussed spirituality, wars, racism, and corruption and to it we added our own thoughts on how to correct the many gross injustices and flaws in society. We were searching for something more than what was being spoon fed to us. One friend was a newscaster who would come over to our house and tell us about reports that came over the wire but couldn't be broadcast. We heard some disturbing reports that were withheld from the public. We knew firsthand to not trust what was being told to the masses. Incidentally, some of these reports can now be found on the internet.

I saw no social boundaries at that time. The community of humanity was on the move; challenging life and transformational possibilities; questioning our role in the universe. In every town there was an open door and lots of serious talking and serious laughing going on. I was at home in the flexibility of thoughts and ideals. I lacked intellectual maturity though and was "all eyes and ears" lacking the brain power to hold on to too much at one time.

And so, it was during this time of high hopes and free thoughts when things in general were full and ripe for me, I stumbled upon the notion of the Kingdom of God. Fool that I was I saw no distance between me and IT. I only knew that IT was my destination. There were several of us that found the concept noteworthy and we discussed the idea with great excitement. It took root in us to different degrees but in all it started us looking for ways of study that were preparatory for our achieving such a noble citizenship.

In particular *Self Awareness* was to be requisite for all self-growth. In short, as we understood it, a Kingdom of God 101 curriculum of study was essential to properly educate an individual in the process of transformation and liberation from the overpowering influence of materialism.

Yes, "The Kingdom of God is within" but without the use of our personal chemistry set, our physical bodies, nothing transforms. The alchemy of self-perfection requires both body and soul; tangible and intangible. This philosophical thought carried through to the necessity of learning the balance between being in the world but not enslaved to it; to be grateful for the beauty of life on earth without losing ourselves to it.

That is a thumbnail description of what I seemed to pluck from the whirlwind of challenges and theories taking place on Planet Earth in those days and if you know anything about those times none of this is something new; I was just one of those fortunate to be born in such "interesting times".

After much reflection and exchange, it was an, "OK what do we do next?" kind of moment. One has to begin somewhere; we needed training; but where would we go to train for entry into the Kingdom of God? Universities or colleges just didn't contain the particular grain of information we were looking for and churches, we felt certain, were holding back. We weren't sure of where to look or what to do but we all committed to looking around to see what might be out there in the world at large.

Within a relatively short period of time after we began our search for schools, my boyfriend, Scott, began talking about a school of continuous education in England. This school was called Sherborne House. Some friends of Scott's were attending the third year course of studies there and after he talked about it a little more, we felt convinced that such a course of study was the type we had been looking for.

We sent off a request for applications for the next year's (4th) course. We didn't know a thing about the curriculum at the time. Scott's friends attending Sherborne were also counter cultural types so we decided to see if this would pan out and be the type of school we were interested in. We received a packet of information and application forms and applied immediately.

In no time after applying we received a call from George C. George was the Alaskan representative for the school. He lived in

Anchorage, which is where Scott and I were living. George was calling to arrange for a meeting with us to discuss our possible acceptance into the fourth year. It was arranged that we would meet George and Mary, his wife, at their house the coming Saturday at 1:00 pm. It was early January by then, 1974.

CHAPTER 5

As our VW bus turned into the snowy driveway, George and Mary popped their heads around the screen door and watched us get out of the car. *This is it*, I thought to myself. I was a little scared by it all but put on a smile. We said our hellos at the door while we stomped the snow from our boots. Once we entered we took off our winter gear of boots and jackets and entered in to their living room. We sat on the couch and George & Mary sat in the two arm chairs.

We spent the afternoon visiting. George asked various questions. Mary made us feel comfortable and invited us to stay for dinner. As they went to church, we stayed back at their home and set the table and kept an eye on the meal that Mary had left simmering on the stove. They came home from church and we shared a pleasant meal together.

During the meeting with George and Mary, George spoke of a Buddhist monk that came to visit Sherborne every year. He taught color meditation and color healing therapy while at Sherborne and George announced to us that we were to work as a group to get the money for Bhante, the monk, to come to Alaska in the summer of 1974. He would introduce us to the meditation while visiting us in Alaska.

Presently color is recognized as an important factor in our environment including the psychological influence it has on our personality and health; but back then the effective uses of color weren't so widely known. In Alaska the colors seemed richer; the hues were strong and vibrant. The lack of color in winter could cause serious problems to a person's psyche-Cabin Fever was a real and dreaded ailment. We were also discovering that, to the trained eye, music vibrates color and chemical analysis through the spectrograph reveals that chemicals emit color relative to the specific chemical. Auras or lights and colors that surround the body are emanations from our own thoughts and attitudes and can reveal the nature of a particular disease.

The first mention of a monk that taught color meditation stirred me; I had had a dream a few weeks before meeting George and Mary which directed me specifically to color. It was a strange sensation hearing George talk about Bhante and color and suddenly remembering the dream. I had forgotten about it by then and it was the farthest thing from my mind when he began talking. I still said nothing to anyone; time would tell, I thought.

We stayed for a little while after dinner to help clean up, then donned our winter gear and said our good-byes. I was glad to see that George and Mary were normal by appearance. I didn't know what to expect but they were two people in their mid to late sixties that had been involved in studies for many, many years. George had met Mary during World War II in England. He was stationed there and Mary was involved with ambulance units. Mary was British and her accent added a worldly note to our conversations. My world had grown tremendously in the little time we spent with them.

On the ride back to our house Scott and I discussed the Brotherhoods, which we understood to be a group of highly evolved humans devoted to the good of mankind. After meeting

George and Mary we were convinced that Sherborne was a school of higher learning. We were amazed that we had found a school so quickly. "Do you think they're Initiates? Is this a school of the Brotherhoods?" We batted thoughts and questions back and forth as we drove home. The mood was lofty as we descended O'Malley Road and turned toward Spenard for home. We were young and so naïve.

CHAPTER 6

A study group was already underway at George and Mary's and within a week after our interview we were incorporated into it. Every generation was represented in the group; with the bulk of us being in our 20's and 30's, mostly hippies all anxious to express and learn.

George and Mary had been associated with the founder of Sherborne, Mr. JG Bennett, since WWII and attended the first course at Sherborne. The group experience was wonderful and as we moved towards spring, then summer we would have work weekends together where we did spring cleaning and garden preparations. We'd leave after tea on Saturday, and then return on Sunday to finish our chores. Some of us cooked while the others performed different tasks assigned by George or Mary. After a few hours, the bell would ring and all would come back to the house, clean up and sit in community for our lunch meal. In the spring it was garden prep and lawn raking; just all kinds of activities around their home. We were a group of free thinkers and many visitors of similar interests or studies came and participated. It was alive and energetic and we made friends for life up there.

As we worked together, we were introduced to exercises that were intended to heighten our perceptions and observe more closely our interactions with others. Here we were introduced to the teachings of GI Gurdjieff. Mr. Gurdjieff had died in 1949 but his teachings lived on in former students such as Mr. Bennett, the founder of Sherborne House. I was not personally drawn to Mr. G's teachings but the challenging observations, community-type living and good hard work was extremely appealing to me.

Mr. Bennett (or Mr. B as he was also called) was a mystical-philosopher type and highly educated in physics. During the many years of his quest for Truth, he had studied with many great spiritual leaders. His aspiration for the school was to provide students an opportunity to have first-hand experience in the various approaches to spiritual practice causing them to discover their own personal potential. Many of these spiritual leaders were able to visit the school and share their wisdom directly with the students. It was never a house of worshipping the guru. True, there are always those that live through someone else's "work" but this was not Mr. B's intention at all. Mr. B was himself a Catholic so it wasn't about rejecting but rather enhancing and it should be noted that the Elders were almost always connected with one of the major religions of the world.

Gurdjieff was the tip of the iceberg in what Mr. Bennett gave to the students at Sherborne House. Mr. Bennett's depth and knowledge was the larger portion of the iceberg; unseen yet all encompassing. I can't say enough about Mr. Bennett and if I tried, I wouldn't do him justice.

Our group chopped and hauled wood and sold it to earn the money for Bhante's airfare. In no time it was summer and Bhante was set to arrive. While Bhante was visiting Alaska, George and Mary's home became a beehive of activity. Bhante had specific time lines he adhered to as a monk and Mary and her helpers prepared his food for timely meals. People came that had heard of his healing powers and wanted some instruction or even a color treatment administered by Bhante. Some from other spiritual disciplines or backgrounds came to talk with him and participate in the evening meditations. People from all over Alaska came to see Bhante. Meditations were held every night and on the weekends a couple of times a day.

We meditated in George and Mary's basement. Green lights replaced the high wattage house lights. They shone down on us as we sat cross legged on the floor, snugly gathered together. A group of about 30 was gathered the first night I meditated. Bhante sat in the middle against the back wall sitting on cushions. Slowly he lit three incense sticks that were standing upright in a vase filled with sand. He waved his hand to extinguish the flame and the sandalwood balsam wafted through the air. The room became still as the green charged smoke encircled our efforts.

Not only was Bhante a meditation master, he had also become a homeopathic physician specializing in color therapy. The color green for the lighting was specific to his teaching that the color green was the harmonizer for humanity and life in general. He pointed out that green was the most prevalent color in nature and had a healing effect on civilization. Green was essential to the life of the planet.

I noticed the air itself seemed charged with a dense invisible quality which was slightly audible. It was truly a comfortable, almost nurturing feeling that I felt when I sat for the first meditation.

After an hour, we ended the meditation, which was followed by a small talk from Bhante and a questions and answer period. Yule asked about purple. He couldn't get the color purple out of his mind as he meditated, while someone else asked several questions about why children die. Bhante laughed with Yule's question and said that purple was a good color and nothing to worry about. He was quiet for some time before he responded to the gentleman's questions about the death of a child. With utmost kindness and respect Bhante replied, "If one can find no reason for the death of a child, then one must accept it as karma." It was apparent that the person asking the questions had lost a loved one. I don't know if it helped in any way, but after his answer all became quiet. We rose and bowed bending slightly at the waist as he left the room. He smiled and said good night. We wished him a good night as well.

When I first saw Bhante, he struck me as a humble person. His presence was not one of electrical hyperactivity but one of solitude. He walked in a radiant silence as though surrounded by a cloud of angels; each step displayed a refined intention. He was a good deal shorter than I was but it was hardly noticeable. As I stood in his presence I felt small and childlike. When he smiled, it was as though a light went on inside of me. His skin was brown and smooth. He was in his eighties but he appeared ageless. He was a master; unnoticeable; energy- not mass.

Meanwhile back at the ranch…Bhante's visit to Alaska was ending and I had not spent any personal time with him or discussed with anyone the dream I had had. I puzzled over this; not really knowing if there was any relationship between the dream's directive towards color and Bhante's appearance in my life. Just a few nods with hello or good-bye were all that was ever exchanged between us.

Saturday, the day before he was to leave, I took the time to spend the day up at George and Mary's house. George was taking Bhante to the Matanuska Valley to see the giant cabbages and other huge vegetables that grew in the rich silt laden soil of the farming community of Palmer. A small group had gathered for the trip but I wasn't one of those going. I stayed behind with Mary. After we had all eaten breakfast I began to help Mary clean up.

Once the group left for the Valley, Mary and I began to talk. I was cleaning the kitchen and Mary was sitting in the dining area, which I could see through the "pass through" above the kitchen sink. Our talk was general until at one point Mary shifted the conversation to my going to Sherborne.

"You don't need to go to Sherborne." She began. "It's damp and cold. It really wouldn't be for you. Bhante is a having a course in India that you should go to. You need to go to India, that way you will have more of a chance of being with the Chosen Ones".

With that said, she handed me a flyer for Bhante's course, which was boldly titled; **Opportunity for Serious Seekers**. I took the flyer and read it. My heart was pounding and only a word here and there registered in my mind. Yes, I will go to India! It was an answer to my inner turmoil. I wasn't sure about England. I wasn't drawn to the Gurdjieff teachings like the others, although I had a great respect for the school. I would have gone to England had this not come about because I knew the education was one that I would benefit from but this new opportunity had presented itself and there was no doubt the moment Mary mentioned this course of study in India, no doubt whatsoever, that India was my destiny and Bhante was truly the Teacher I was to learn from.

I stayed at George and Mary's all day waiting for the group with Bhante to return. He was leaving the next day and I didn't know what might be required of me in speaking to him about his course of study. When they returned, I requested to speak with Bhante in private. Bhante was staying in the back bedroom at the end of the hallway. Slowly I walked back and lightly tapped on his door. He said "Come in." and I entered. Bhante was sitting to my left in an armchair. He pointed to another chair and invited me to sit down. Once I settled in to the chair Bhante asked, "Now, what can I do for you?" I began to explain about the talk Mary and I had and how I had learned about his course in India and that I would like to be on that course. Bhante sat quietly and listened to me. After a long moment of silence he asked me seriously, "Now, why do you want to attend the course?" Something tumbled out about the meditations I had been to at George and Mary's and my experiences in them. I never mentioned the dream; I kept that to myself as was often the case for me.

After my explanation, I glanced up to see Bhante laughing; all he said was, "Sure, you can come!" Relief and exhilaration flooded over me.

I jumped up and said, "Thank you!" I believe I also hugged him without thinking about it. I was going to India in the fall to attend Bhante's first and only course of Color Meditation and Color healing.

"If one person can benefit from this effort, then I will consider it a success." That was the last statement of the flyer. "If just one person can benefit..."

CHAPTER 7

The next few months were spent working and saving money for the journey and going to group activities at George and Mary's. Scott and I had broken up. We still saw each other through the activities and he was still going to Sherborne. It was just like that back then; a lot of break ups and make ups and get togethers. I had already applied for my passport so that was crossed off the list. I thought long and hard on what to pack. What does one pack for a 5-6 month stay in India? I had only a small knapsack that would have to contain all the things I felt important or necessary for traveling and living in general.

During this time as well, I had received a postcard from Bhante inviting me to join him and several others in driving to India. There was room and they needed drivers. I found an ad in 17 Magazine that stated the importance of an international driver's license so I had applied for it. Cross that off the list and Yes, to Bhante's invitation to accompany them on the drive. I wrote him a quick letter expressing how happy I was to accompany him and the others on the drive. The international driver's license arrived in plenty of time; I later found out it wasn't all that necessary but it sounded impressive to send off for something so worldly.

My imagination ran wild with anticipation as thoughts to the long drive ahead of me lay on the horizon. Adventure of the most incredible nature was taking shape and I allowed myself to be pulled by its current. It was a mix of joy and fear. The unknown appealed to me and this fast moving-fast unfolding "Opportunity for Serious Seekers" had a force of its own. Leaving Alaska, leaving everything, *that* was difficult. Change didn't scare me; it was the process of changing that frightened me. I worked and saved, worked and saved.

When the time came to leave, it was difficult to say good-bye to friends. I hadn't taken any time to study any geography maps or cultural digests on the various countries that I would be driving through. For that matter, I had no idea what countries we would be driving through. I received bits of advice from world travelers. The most helpful back in 1974, which I did apply, was "Say you are from Alaska. Most of them have never heard of it and they won't know you are American. They hate Americans." This worked on several occasions in particular during my stay in England.

"Where are you from?"

"Alaska."

"Alaska, where is that?"

"Oh, it's next to Canada."

Worked every time…

I had a little send-off party at my dad's house and stayed at my best friend Suzie's house the night before I left. The next morning Suzie took me to breakfast and gave me a wrist watch for the trip. I cried a little at the breakfast and she asked me what I was crying about. I told her I didn't know and that I was scared. She looked at me like I was an idiot. She wished she could do it. By this time Suzie had a child and husband and travel was out. It was a good send off for me. What was the problem? Absolutely nothing...

It was September, 1974 when I left Alaska. Molly H picked me up at Heathrow Airport outside of London. I had met Molly that spring when she came to visit the group. She was English and we had struck up a friendship of sorts during her visit. She was extremely helpful and offered a room for me in her cottage while I waited for Bhante. Her cottage was in the village of Sherborne not far from the school. Another family was also staying there at her cottage while she was living in London. No one knew where Bhante was, she told me; she assured me he would pop up sooner or later.

Thank heavens for her kindness. I had only heard from Bhante once after accepting his offer to drive with him to India. What he wrote to me the last time was something to the effect that he hoped to leave the UK in early September to make the overland drive. No one else I knew would be going to India. I would meet a whole new group all with their own history.

Once we arrived at Molly's cottage I met her other houseguests. The young lady was pregnant and I think had at least one other child. I can't remember meeting her husband but she made it quickly clear that she had no interest in getting to know me. So that was that, and that was all there was to it. The "I'm from Alaska" line had no effect on her.

Molly stayed to visit for a little while. She had to get back to London before dark and she left sooner than I had hoped. My friends who were scheduled for the 4th year hadn't arrived yet; I was alone. I climbed the steps to my bedroom and stayed there; I just parked myself there and during any given day when it became quiet downstairs I would pop out of my "den". I would go down the stairs, bathe, and maybe make a hot cup of instant coffee. I didn't dare eat any of their food. It was a lonely existence and my unworldliness radiated outward in the form of a constant blush.

Bathed and dressed, I would then go outside to take a nice long walk. I loved England instantly. The town of Sherborne was quiet. There were hills and dales and stone hedges lined the sidewalk. The cottages were off the road behind the stone hedge a good 20 feet or so. I could walk and take my time to glance at the homes without feeling intrusive. Everything seemed so tidy. What a wonderful place. On the one hand I ached for home and on the other I just loved this newness of cultures and landscapes. Smells of grass and dampness filled the air and on the waterway swans were swimming; it was picture perfect.

After walking about half a mile I found a small shop that sold everything from gossip rags to Pepto-Bismol. I was so hungry, yet I didn't know what to eat. I was beyond thinking about food. I was tired and hungry and couldn't focus. I wasn't sure what utensils were back at Molly's and the labels were not labels I was used to. I purchased one orange and a chocolate bar. I ate the orange quickly and suffered the pain of eating the wrong food on an empty stomach. The citrus hitting my belly created a churning and rumbling; I hunched over a little and held on to my stomach. Not only that, I had left Alaska with a cold and my ears had not depressurized from the trip. I had tried everything from chewing gum to gulping down water but nothing popped my ears. It was painful but most of all it left me feeling that I was in a dream state. As I blew my nose copious amounts of blood would come out. I was miserable; walking around with plugged ears and hunger. I didn't eat for days.

Finally, Don and Roberta showed up from Alaska to attend the fourth year at Sherborne School. We were all part of the group at George and Mary's and also Don and Roberta were lifelong friends of Scott's. Our families all went back to the pioneering

days of Alaska. Roberta was an angel-a true friend. I can still see
her sweet face as she and Don visited with me. I think we were all
scared but didn't say so. They came to Molly's cottage whenever
they were free; they had come a full two weeks early for the course
but had chores to do almost instantly back at Sherborne House.
Scott hadn't come to England yet but was still scheduled for the
fourth year course. Still no Bhante...

Then one day; I heard footsteps followed by a knock at my
door. It was the lady of the house. "Come quickly, Bhante is here."
I jumped out of bed and ran down the stairs.

There he was; alive and real before my eyes. He was sitting
on the couch in his orange robes and smiling, of course always
smiling. "There, see, nothing to worry about," said Pierre Elliott.
Pierre was on staff at Sherborne House at the time and had
brought Bhante to the cottage.

Bhante welcomed me and explained where he had been and
what had delayed him. I didn't hear a word he said. All I knew was
that he was finally here and if I could have, I would have shouted,
"Come on, let's get the Hell out of here!" Instead I just smiled and
nodded with my feet glued to the floor.

We would leave tomorrow morning. Presently, Bhante said
he would be spending some time with Mr. B back at Sherborne.
They left, and I went upstairs and gathered up my possessions. I
sat and sat and sat on my bed waiting for the hours to pass. I was
ready to put this leg of the journey behind me.

CHAPTER 8

Early the next morning, Bhante arrived by car to pick me up. I had already bathed and had been waiting for some time. I was introduced to Duff and William, who was owner and driver of the car we were in. Both of them would be making the drive to India to be on the course as well.

I hopped into the car and we exchanged the usual good mornings and how do you do. The next thing Bhante said was, "First we must eat." Whew! Food! I was so happy. *How did he know I hadn't eaten and was near starvation?*

He directed William to find the nearest restaurant. Once we were seated, Duff helped me with the small menu. "You must try Bangers" said Duff. They are a plump pork sausage and saying they are juicy and full of flavor is an understatement. Wow, my first bite of solid food in at least a week -- less one orange and one chocolate bar. I ordered Bangers, scrambled eggs, toast with marmalade and lots of hot freshly brewed coffee. I would live another day.

Bhante was a vegetarian and I wondered if it was respectful for me to eat meat in his presence. I also worried about gobbling up my portions like a starving dog. I had to find the balance -- I guess the *middle path* in eating etiquette. *Chew slowly, smile, no, for heaven's sake don't smile, chew slowly, be friendly, no, don't talk with food in your mouth, don't gulp,* my inner dialogue was screaming at me as I concerned myself with how I looked, how I ate and was food stuck in my teeth. I managed not to appear ravenous and still eat a huge portion of everything available.

What a sight; an elderly orange-robed Buddhist monk sitting with three hippies stuffing their faces on bangers and scrambled eggs. Oh, the fun and excitement of the hippie days! Freedom to eat with a Buddhist monk in a small restaurant without any consideration... Now, in this *Brave New World* things are quite different.

We drove to London where Duff had made arrangements with a young lady to let me stay in her flat while we gathered the necessary gear for our drive. Her name was Polly.

We went to a house that was owned by a group of Sherborne students, perhaps even Mr. B or his family; I am not sure now. People were coming and going -- it had that kind of energy. I met Polly in the kitchen area where she was cooking liver in a frying pan on the gas stove. She was friendly and spoke with a British accent. I was surprised to learn that she was an American and had been on a previous year at Sherborne and was staying in London for awhile. *I get it -- I'm from Alaska and she's got an accent-blending; no one will ever know we are stupid Americans.* She had a flat in London and I was welcome to stay there. Someone called out to her and off she ran up the stairs. She left the meat cooking and I sat and waited for her thinking, *OK any minute she will return and finish cooking.* She didn't return and soon the liver was smoking. I got up and tended to the burning liver not really knowing what to do but making sure there wasn't a fire started while I waited for her to come back. She returned after a while and went on cooking without noticing the charred liver; talking about her flat, where she was working and how she wasn't home that often and I was welcome to stay with her. I got the key and my ride took me to her flat.

Her flat, which was someplace in London, was on the second floor. The kitchen was outside the flat off to the right and was shared with two young men whose flat was on the third floor. The bathroom was in the basement. It was a tiny bathroom with the usual coin operated water heater. With all the going ups and downs I saw the two young men only once as they were leaving the kitchen. They were nice and we talked a little to one another. They were students at some college in the city.

Her place was one large room with a fire place and modest furnishings. It had the air of a busy tenant with clothes hanging over a dressing screen, shoes laying in several places, jewelry here and there on various end tables. Although untidy, it was comfortable and clean. She usually came home and rushed out and we didn't cross paths much.

During my stay in London at the flat I was able to do some sightseeing; just the usual places such as Big Ben, the Thames, and Buckingham Palace. Most of all was the food, how I loved the food in the small shops that sold their particular specialty products.

In all my roaming and wondering I was discovering all kinds of new foodstuffs; McVitee's Chocolate covered digestives, a wonderful wheat biscuit topped with chocolate, wonderful hot and strong coffee infused with steamed milk. I couldn't get enough of that stuff. It was the first time I had ever seen coffee made with such precision and what flavor! I would watch the steam as it hissed and bubbled through the mixture to just the right temperature. It was perfection. They did not have this in Alaska. The most thrilling thing about coffee in Alaska was the camp coffee my dad showed me how to make. You throw ground coffee into a pot of boiling water and after a few minutes you crack a raw egg over the top. The egg draws the grounds down to the bottom. What you get is mud and this ugly lump at the bottom that resembles a dead rat.

I did a lot of walking and sitting; drinking the café coffee and sending mega postcards; my homesickness satisfied and my gypsy spirit fed at the same time. I also found some wonderful Indian restaurants and tasted the most fantastic Southern India curry, which made me more anxious to taste curry in India.

Bhante was staying at a Buddhist Monastery/House in London and I would take a cab or walk to see him from Polly's flat. When Bhante's devotees found out he was at the monastery, they began to come prepare his meals and visit with him. He would spend quite a bit of his afternoon visiting with guests that had come to pay their respects. The first day I visited Bhante he opened the outer door for me and as we made preparation to enter the monastery area he talked to me a little about how to address a monk.

"Bring your hands together and bow slightly, like so. You must also bow to the monk when you enter and leave a room. I am just telling you this because I see that you do not know these things." He showed great humility in his instructions to me. I listened to every word hoping I would get it right.

Mike Sutton was visiting and cooking for Bhante the first day I came to visit. He had brought massive quantities of celery, which was Bhante's favorite vegetable. I met Mike through the kitchen door where he was madly cooking away and talking excitedly. He smiled and waved a stalk of celery in my direction. I liked Mike instantly. He was friendly and welcoming. He had a bon vivant energy that was infectious to the point where I found myself smiling without knowing why. He just gave off this wonderful confident and joyful energy.

When I left that day, I did a robotic bow to the monks, worrying about whether I had bowed deeply enough or if I should bend more. It was a, *Yes, that's good enough; no wait maybe just a little more* jerking type bending/bowing motion. I looked at Bhante, he was smiling at me. I knew he could see how confused I was. Others that knew him and were familiar with Buddhism protocol would show great reverence and I felt pretty lost in what to do. It didn't matter though, as long as one made the effort and showed respect; I was learning as I went along.

On another day, I went to visit Bhante and pay my tuition for the course. It was $450.00 for the entire course; including room and board. *Damn cheap* as Bhante would say. I had gone to the bank earlier and cashed in some travelers checks. They gave me the whole amount for the tuition in one or five pound notes. I wasn't familiar enough with how currency exchanges went so I took the bundles of small notes and stuffed them into my knapsack and walked the few remaining blocks to where Bhante was staying. When I gave the money to him I noticed how he looked at it strangely and I fretted that I had misunderstood the cost and not paid enough so I said "$450.00 dollars?" (I think it was $450.00)

He smiled and said "Yes, yes".

I wasn't a person who planned things. I just never thought of things like; maybe just several American one hundred dollar bills would have done the trick. I could have taken care of this task in Alaska but it never crossed my mind. So he was stuck with a suitcase full of one or five pound notes. He didn't laugh or ask me to go back and get larger notes and it wasn't until later I realized what I had done; the American dollar was the preferred currency in those days (1.79 to the British pound as I recall). I just plain didn't think things through at times. On the one hand, that was good; it brought me on this journey; on the other hand what the heck was I thinking?

As a side note; this is how Bhante was as a teacher. He never purposely caused me humiliation. He could get angry at me for what I thought were small things where the big things that were life-changing; he said nothing. This incident is not in itself life-changing but observation of my lack of forethought haunted me for years before the *DUHHHHH* kicked in.

CHAPTER 9

Our stay in London was brief. I had spent some wonderful days walking and bussing around the city and was really enjoying London and its people. But in the middle of the night not more than a week after arriving, Polly telephoned me and said to get ready to leave. I packed up my belongings and went down the flight of stairs to the street below. It was dark when the Morris Minor minivan pulled up. Bhante was next to the driver and all the rest, including Polly, were piled into the back. I went to the back door and climbed on board. In the quiet darkness of the drive I could hear Bhante speaking harshly about "those monks".

We came to find out they had asked him to leave. They simply could not tolerate all the westerners coming and going; they thought it best he find new living accommodations. I was a bit shocked at this but I was a westerner and the coming and going was fine with me. I knew I wasn't too great at bowing and all that stuff but the rest seemed to know how to behave. Oh well, just another leg of the journey ending and a new one beginning. Off we drove taking the first ramp available on to the freeway and heading to parts unknown, at least to me.

Bhante was at home with Westerners. He was enthusiastic about the changes taking place all over the world and the interests of the hippies. Many times he said "What I am, anyone can become." He never forgot who he was and where he came from. When he would discuss his family he was incredibly humble and did not place significance on social standings. What was important to him was the opportunity to share the experience and not setting himself apart from any person.

"I wasn't always like this."

"When I was young, I had no cares. I drank; I smoked and drove a fancy car. It was the custom in Cambodia that before a man could marry; he had to commit to being a monk for a certain amount of time. I had not done that. I lived a continental life and did not know anything about the Buddha. I was already married and had a child when I made my commitment and entered into the monastery. The longer I stayed, the more curious I became. The people would come and leave all kinds of valuable things in homage to the Buddha; they fed us and bowed to us. I wondered who this Buddha was. Why were the people so devoted to this person? I felt ashamed and knew that I had to find out who was the Buddha. I decided to become a monk 100%. I was the same age as Lord Buddha was when I left my family, even having a newborn child like the Buddha, but I knew it was what I had to do."

So what some Buddhist monks found unsettling; Bhante saw nothing wrong with. He knew what his past was and saw the potential for change in all people.

We arrived at our host's, the Myat Shi's estate, within an hour and a half from when we started out in London. In the dark there wasn't much to see. We made a turn into the driveway and immediately stopped the car. We were at a gatehouse. Bhante was dropped off there. He was expected so another monk greeted him at the door. Once Bhante was taken care of we continued to go up the paved driveway. We went to the right side and around a huge mansion. I couldn't get the full impact of the residence in the dark but its large silhouette against the starry sky let me know it was not a house of small stature.

I was dropped off in the back and Duff pointed for me to take the stairs to the second level. The stairs were on the outside so I got out of the car and climbed the steps to my new digs. Since I was expected, the door was unlocked. I gently opened the door and went in. I stood at the doorway scanning the area. As I stepped in, the floor creaked a little and I held back for a moment hoping that I wasn't waking anyone up. There was a small light on the stair landing that illuminated the small space so I decided not to turn on any inside lights.

Straight ahead, there was a small kitchen with appliances and a tiny dining table with two chairs. I tip toed around checking out the rooms to find a bedroom. The WC was to the right of the kitchen and there was a bedroom across from it. I returned to the door and faced the kitchen; to the left I spotted another bedroom.

I chose the small room to the left of the kitchen and threw my gear on the bed. I quickly unrolled my sleeping bag and changed into some cotton long johns for sleeping. There was a coin operated heater near the bed. It was a bit chilly so I plunked some coins into the slot. Being used to central heating, I expected the heat to just pop out and fill the room instantly -- not the case here; the heat took its time to make a small dent to the chilly room. I got into bed, leaned over and turned on the small radio that was on the night stand and found a station playing Olivia Newton John. *Good enough*, I thought. I tucked myself in for the night, said a small prayer and fell to sleep.

The next morning, there was a knock at the door. I was already up and dressed when I answered it. Mrs. Myat Shi, the hostess of the property had come to introduce herself to me. Her family, who were from Burma, owned the large estate that I was now staying in. We talked a little about the accommodations and

I was told that they were free for anyone traveling with the monk. She was right to the point about things. We didn't exchange pretentious pleasantries but she was a beautiful woman with kind features. Her husband who, seemed quite a bit older than she, was an entrepreneur in the import/export business. She was lady of the house and was responsible for the mansion's upkeep and saw to the care of the monks. They had two daughters, both equally beautiful.

At the time, there was just one monk living on the property in the gatehouse. He was attending college in Oxford. I was to be responsible for caring for him as well as Bhante while I was staying there. It would be my duty to prepare the meals for the monks. They ate breakfast by 8:00 a.m. and their lunch meal was to be prepared and served by 11: 30 am. Buddhist monks did not eat after their lunchtime meal. I had no clue as to what to cook for them but I said "OK". Breakfast had already been served to them so I would start with lunch preparation. After our hostess left I set about seeing what was in the kitchen. I discovered a box on the kitchen table that contained a bag of lentils and some carrots and onions. Some of the vegetables were shriveled but I decided to make a lentil soup. I was nervous about all this.

First and foremost as I said before, I wasn't a person who planned things. Yes, I could cook but never from a recipe. I learned to cook from example or inspiration; not training, and it was always "a little of this, a little of that" meal prep. I really wasn't a cook and secondly what do you feed monks?? I was nervous about this because I felt terribly inadequate in serving them. Nevertheless, I made the soup and by 11:15 or so I was walking down the driveway to the gatehouse carrying the pan of hot soup.

I knocked on the Gatehouse door. I was so frightened when Bhante opened the door to me. "So, what have you prepared for us?" he asked.

I told him "lentil soup" and lifted the lid to show him the contents. Bhante looked down into the pan then smiled, bidding me to enter. I met the other young monk who was from Ceylon (Sri Lanka) as I passed through to the kitchen via the living room/dining room area. I set the soup on the stove and searched around for utensils, plates, bowls, drinking glasses, etc. I glanced into the fridge and found some juice. I found the teapot and put water on for tea. I just had to wing it and hope for the best. I set the dining table in the living room and called them to lunch. I did not eat with them; I waited in the kitchen peeking out once in a while to see if they were eating or needed anything else. I was happy to see that they were eating; *phew, this crisis has passed!* I gave out a sigh and quietly closed the door.

When the meal was over, Bhante came into the kitchen. "Tomorrow, you come early. I will teach you how to cook".

"OK", I replied.

Well, at least I would be learning to cook him the food he preferred. I wasn't at all offended by this. I was relieved in fact. I made my good-byes for the day and went back up to my room.

It seemed a long walk up that hill. Now that it was daylight, I took time to view the mansion. It was a large three-story structure that to me should have been in the Bavarian Alps. It was a dark brown wooden chateau structure with all kinds of fancy wood carvings and tall windows. My goodness, this was wealth personified! Coming from Alaska as I had, this was over the top in luxury. There was a large entryway into the mansion; all glass and doors with heavy clay pots filled with tall shrubbery flanking the entry way. Through the entry doors, I could see a wide and open elegant staircase going up to the second level. Not wanting to stand and gawk, I took in as much as I could as I ascended the hillside. We were surrounded by large trees that enfolded the property. The whole of the hillside directly in front of the chalet was beautiful, neatly mowed, rich green grass. The driveway appeared to have been newly paved with not one bump or break in the clean dark pavement. The whole of the estate was immaculate.

I went right and skirted around the mansion to the back steps up to my room. I felt alone and now Duff and William were gone as well. I was told that Duff had left for the Continent to purchase the autos for the drive to India. It was lonely and once again I was left with a sense of "what next" jitters. I hadn't spent any time with Bhante and although I knew I was where I should be, the idea of being in his esteemed presence and being taught to cook by *him* caused me to make some mental notes like: wear your deodorant tomorrow and your bra, take your shoes off at the door, be sure to have on clean socks -- no holes. I once again performed a mental litany of dos and don'ts and God help me's for tomorrow's cooking lesson. How embarrassing that an elderly Buddhist monk had to teach *me* how to cook. I shrugged to myself as I pondered tomorrow's affair. It was a tough job but somebody had to do it.

Mrs. Myat Shi came by to check on how everything had gone for the day. I told her everything seemed to go well. She was genuinely surprised when I told her that I didn't know anything about tending to a monk. She explained a few helpful sets of rules for serving monks. Monks were never to be touched, one always bows when entering and when leaving, shoes off, place food on a table; do not hand them their food, etc. She was a devoted Buddhist and felt she could not do enough for the monks. Every action done to accommodate the monk was good Karma for the family, she told me. Every day she would leave a box at my door with vegetables and other food items. From that, I was to prepare the daily meals. There was no menu just the box. She warmed up to me after she learned that I was accompanying Bhante to India to attend his course and that I had never been to Europe before. We ended up becoming close and she was a tremendous help in all things Buddhist.

CHAPTER 10

The next morning, I was up early to go down to prepare their breakfast and then to learn to prepare the lunch meal. I carried the box down with me and took it straight to the kitchen. There were also some eggs and bread in the kitchen so I decided on eggs, tea and toast. There was a lot of fresh garlic on the counter and I also noticed some green peppers. I moved all the food items about on the counter; feeling the weight of the garlic, seeing if the bread felt hard or soft, was there butter, and was the butter soft? Just generally rummaging around and getting comfortable.

I wondered about those green peppers; were they the sweet green peppers, which would be good in an omelet that I was used to eating or were these hot peppers, which I had heard of but never seen or tasted? They weren't large like the sweet green peppers I knew from back home but they weren't little either so I just didn't know what they were. Curiosity got the best of me and I thought, *oh what the heck, I'll just take a pinch of one and see what it is.* Holy crap! It was a burning hot pepper that just exploded in my throat. I did a gallop and a whinny as the flames hit my stomach. I was absolutely panicked at the heat and now look at the time I was losing; I have to get breakfast ready and I'm gagging! Without thinking, I rubbed my cheeks and they ignited -- a few more minutes lost in the cooking. I tried to spit as much out in the sink as I could but the burn simmered within. I was terrified and wondered do I wash my hands off with soap and water or sprinkle baking soda on them? Do I rinse my mouth out? I had no idea and I was scared I would miss that all critical 8:00 deadline. I performed a left to right pass off motion trying to decide what to do. I went for the cold water and grabbing the dish soap, I washed my hands and rinsed thoroughly.

I took great care not to contaminate the morning meal or burn any other part of my body. I had to chop, plop and cook without my fingers touching any of the food. My heart was beating in my chest as I cautiously moved around trying to prepare the breakfast meal.

Everything was so new to me that each effort seemed to set off a five-alarm emotion inside of me and then my mind would just go blank. But this too passed and the first breakfast ever prepared for Bhante by me went off without missing the all too critical timeline. *Thank heavens I wore my deodorant today.* I thought to myself. The heat from the peppers and my body temperature made me sweat profusely and soon he would be coming in to teach *me* to cook.

Just after I had cleaned the breakfast dishes and straightened up the dining area, Bhante came into the kitchen. He proceeded to inspect the food and we began my first class. He took the vegetables and began to show me how to cut up each one. "Do not peel the vegetables, you may clean them of debris and dirt but leave the skins on." Each vegetable had to be cut just so and put into the hot oiled pan at just the right time. Each vegetable group was separated from the other and as we began to cook, he showed me which one should be cooked first, second and so on. He also put the water on for rice and measured out the water to rice ratio with a slow, intentional effort. He spoke kindly and did not show any impatience at my inexperience. I made every effort to show respect and I knew that he could tell I was ignorant but not stupid. I slowly chopped each vegetable, making sure that each one had the same thickness to allow an even cooking. What a special time that was for me. He took me under his wing and kindly and carefully trained me in cooking for him. His movements were measured and precise. No energy was lost in his cooking; a clove of garlic chopped, just so, was an epiphany.

After that, and on most of the days, Bhante would come into the kitchen to see what I was preparing and offer advice. He showed me how to make his favorite tea, which was jasmine with chopped ginger.

"Just a pinch of the tea," he told me and he would put his hand into the box and bring out between his thumb and index finger a small thimbleful of the jasmine mix, "The water must boil vigorously then quickly poured into the tea pot. Sprinkle the small dry tea over the water and put the chopped ginger in next. Leave it to brew, do not stir. It should smell light with the full fragrance of the flower dominating the senses. The ginger should be tasted but not overwhelm the scent of the light jasmine." Bhante would lift the lid and wave the steamy fragrance in my direction. He liked honey in his tea and I got adept at adding just the right amount for him into his teacup.

He loved celery and I made sure that it was in almost every meal I made for him. "Don't peel the ribs of the celery because it is a healthy part of the stalk and contains fiber. Add the thin cuts of the celery at the end of the cooking to keep it crunchy and sweet. Never should the vegetables be soft, always leaving a slight crunch."

At times, Mrs. Myat Shi came with special foods from her native land, Burma. Bhante especially enjoyed it when she brought her dishes. Mrs. Myat Shi would take time to explain and show me the dishes she had prepared and would demonstrate the proper presentation of food to a monk. She and her daughters would arrive; first, shoes off, then making bows to the monks and speaking words of veneration. Bhante would say a few words to respond. This was all in Burmese; Bhante spoke many languages. They brought pastel enameled tin bowls that stacked one on top of the other in a stackable carrying case along with handle. I had never seen one before. It was impressive. I was so green about almost everything that any discovery of a new cooking device, receptacle or flavor filled me with great pleasure. Slowly they put each piping hot bowl on the table and lifted the lids one at a time. The aromas that misted out of those pots were divine. Each dish was presented to Bhante. They then set about serving and bowing. It was an elaborate and reverent affair that was art in itself. Without words or clanging and banging a lovely meal was set before the monks.

Chapter 11

Once lunch was served to the monks, I would eat in the kitchen. After they had eaten, I would clean up. The afternoons began to get full with letter writing and other tasks for Bhante. He had a lot of correspondence and an occasional visitor which required me to prepare tea and a small snack for the guest. We grew so synchronized that without a word to me, I would know when to fetch his glasses on the side table or draw a curtain for light or for shade; just little things but much we were in tune with each other and the time went quickly and smoothly. We began to talk about family or traveling. He was so genuine and unassuming that I loved being around him. He had a keen sense of humor and was witty, not unlike me. We could laugh together; sometimes to tears.

My association with Bhante quickly changed from stranger to trusted elder. I had grown comfortable with him and could be myself. Quite frankly, I had never experienced such a familiarity with any elder before this. I was extremely grateful for his kindness.

Some days were just quiet and peaceful. I had fed the monks, the one monk had gone to his room and Bhante and I would sit without conversation. Many times this was how an opportunity for him to speak to me came about.

"I could hear a leaf drop to the ground... When I lived in the forests of Thailand I could hear life in everything."

I listened; never an intense listening but a peaceful listening such as to the grass when a soft wind tickles its tiny blades. The story was the moment and I seemed to see, smell and hear his experience. He could hear a leaf as it removed itself from the tree and gently float down to lightly rest on the forest floor. He did not have to see the leaf to know it had arrived safely on the ground. I loved the stories he would tell.

The time came when he left his forest retreat forever. In the forests of Thailand, he and several other monks had committed to an oath of silence and there they lived for six or so years. Every day one or all of the monks would enter a nearby village and beg for their daily food. "Into the alms pot went everything imaginable and we had to eat it just the way it was placed in the pot-without discretion. This was how we fed ourselves! Then, one day a man came to me. His wife was dying and he had heard we were living in the forest near his village. He asked me to come and see to his wife. When I got there I could see his wife was near death. I extended my hand to her, not touching her, but reaching my hand towards her. Instantly I felt a force move through me and enter her dying body. She was instantly healed. After that, word spread about the healing and I was forced to return to the world."

That was how he ended up coming out of the forest leaving his vow of silence and reentering society. It was a bit sad for me to hear. In many ways I knew he missed those years of forest living.

Chapter 12

Then one day Ron showed up. He was the other American who would be driving with us to India. I had been starving for company so his presence was greatly appreciated. I enjoyed talking with him and we began to both do the cooking and cleaning. I usually stayed after with Bhante when he wanted assistance. We didn't spend much private time together but Ron was a great guy and funny. How did he know Bhante? He didn't. He found the flyer stapled to a telephone pole in his home town and decided to call the number on it. That was it, he called the number and here he was. That was just how it worked. Ron had a bouncy step. He walked/hopped on the balls of his feet which defined his character. He always was smiling or laughing and his belief was that all should love one another. He had brought a recorder with him and often at night he would play wistful notes that floated to my bedroom. They were comforting tunes; putting me to sleep almost instantly. He was about five feet eleven, had black hair, jolly brown eyes and a full beard. He wore the eastern pajama pants and loose shirts and was already halfway to India before we had left England.

One night, Ron and I went into the nearby village of Botley for coffee. We got to laughing about things in general and returned to the estate a little later than expected. We had been sitting at a café when the local cross dresser came up to the window in front of us and began to adjust his bra, apply lipstick and grab his crotch to adjust God only knows what. The fellow was well known for his antics and did this performance at most tourists' haunts; we just happened to be in the right place at the right time and the whole event was captivating.

Bhante was waiting up for us and the sideways glance he gave me let me know he didn't approve of my being out at this hour of the night with a man. He felt personally responsible for me and didn't want any harm to come to me. It was the first time Bhante was cross with me and it cut me to the core. I tried not to displease him again. He was also cross because unbeknownst to us, Duff had returned with two vehicles for the drive; a large gray Mercedes van and a green VW bus. Duff was a little apologetic about the two weeks it had taken him to find the cars. He had spent all the money and the car's titles were missing.

"Oh that fellow, oh that fellow..." Bhante kept repeating and shaking his head. Duff was in the dog house for sure. I didn't quite get the dilemma but I knew Duff's arrival meant we would be leaving for India soon.

I really loved our stay on the Myat Shi's estate. I had gotten to know Bhante and felt close to him and I had become well acquainted with Mrs. Myat Shi on a personal level. She spoke often of her concern for Bhante; taking on such a long drive at his age. In one of our conversations she told me that she had asked Bhante why, at his age, was he taking on such a huge project; driving and then conducting a course? He told her that it was his task to teach this specific group of people. It was obvious to her that he was on a special mission but at the same time she was a little perplexed that we weren't necessarily Buddhist or Asian.

When the time to leave was at hand, Mrs. Myat Shi and I went in to Oxford to shop for the drive. She was insistent on supplying food for our long journey. We selected bags of rice; large glass jars of digestives, tins of jam, black tea, sugar and honey, soy sauce; all kinds of food items, which she preceded to purchase. The family's generosity would be enough to last the whole drive and then some. This was an important part of her being Buddhist. A right action, she explained to me, especially to a monk of high stature, was good karma. She asked me to please remind Bhante from time to time so that he would remember her family. Of course he remembered her and they maintained a close friendship until Bhante died.

CHAPTER 13

We were already behind schedule; waiting for the vehicles had caused a serious delay and Bhante did not want to wait another minute to get on the road. Duff came and picked us up in one of the vehicles. William had the other vehicle and was waiting for us in London. We didn't pack the van too well when we left. It was more a throw your gear in and let's get-going pace. We said our good-byes and thank you all to everyone on hand and headed for London.

Our first stop in London was at a house sale. Someone knew one of the sons of the household; I believe it was a Sherborne connection. There were several single mattresses and other items that Bhante wanted to buy to bring to the monastery. Bhante and the young man of the house along with Duff and William walked throughout the rooms looking through the items. Bhante haggled for the mattresses and got them. That poor young man; how could he haggle with Bhante? You could see it on his face; he was completely helpless to Bhante's suggestions and wore a worried expression which reflected a, *what am I going to tell my parents when they come home and find that I sold the lot for a cheap -- damn cheap price?*

All of the mattresses and other household items and all of our personal gear, food and miscellaneous stuff were crammed into the Mercedes van. Bhante had taken over the back of the VW. It was a camper so the sleeping area was his domain. He wasn't happy how everything was packed and announced that we would repack once we were in France.

We left the house and went to the home of Karen. She had invited Bhante over for a farewell gathering and meditation. It was getting later now and we had to get to Dover to catch the ferry in time for the crossing to Calais, France. I met a few others, Adam and Gunther who were also going on the course and driving with us.

Gunther's girlfriend had come to attend the meditation and send off. It was not planned for her to come with us. Charlotte was a pretty young blonde lady. We were all so young and I hesitate to use the word lady or man for any of us-we were still children. I was 24 at the time and she was even younger. I look at my children now in their mid-twenties and wonder, *my goodness, was I that young when I went to India? Did I look that young?* The answer to that is, yes, I did.

After the meditation Gunther and Charlotte were sitting near Bhante when Bhante turned to Gunther and asked him if he wanted her to come.

Gunther said, "Yes, I would like that!" Bhante then turned to Charlotte and asked her if she wanted to come.

She replied, "Yes."

"Then come!" was all Bhante said.

Charlotte ran home to pack. She returned within the hour with a small brown suitcase. There we were, and of course, Bhante, all together now and finishing our stay in England.

All of those present were associated with Sherborne or Mr. B in one way or another. Adam was sixteen going on about thirty. He didn't want to continue with his schooling and instead elected to be on the course with us and accompany us on the drive. His parents were on staff at Sherborne.

He was young but possessed a great maturity and a healthy respect for Bhante. We, each of us, didn't know each other well but most had a direct link with Sherborne and then Ron and I had been tending to Bhante so there was a familiarity that ran through the gathering. It extinguished any apprehension we had towards one another. Granted we would get to know each other better but one thin crystallized layer of "getting to know you" was shaved away.

Karen bid us good-bye along with her best wishes and we began our drive. It was dark and raining when we took off. William and Duff drove the vehicles. I didn't get to see much in this drive being once again a mad dash to another destination in the dark. We arrived in Dover just in time to board the autos and ourselves.

We boarded the ferry and our nighttime Channel crossing began. Bhante stayed in the VW while the rest of us roamed the upper deck. Again too dark to see anything outside, we took to the duty free stores and the wooden benches. Charlotte and Gunther strolled around the deck together. Charlotte was wearing a vintage fur coat that came to her knees and Gunther had on a black turtleneck with jeans. They resembled a couple right out of the *Maltese Falcon*. As the light hit their serious faces along with their attire I felt I had journeyed back in time.

I don't think any of us slept that night or at least not soundly. The benches were hard and uncomfortable and there was nothing to look out on being that it was nighttime. After about an hour, the duty free shop had lost its appeal; I wish I could say, "In no time, we arrived in Calais" but I can't. It was a long, dark night that I clearly remember.

CHAPTER 14

Finally, Calais at sunrise! We drove the vehicles off the ferry and drove over to the small gas station. There was a small shop and restrooms. I popped into the toilet facilities for a quick washing down and brushing of my teeth.

We hadn't discussed the trip with each other. I certainly knew nothing about getting to India but Duff knew the direction and I didn't question it. Duff let us know that we weren't going near Paris; we would be heading across and over to Switzerland. Off we went.

It was almost surreal as we accelerated the autos and moved forward. We found the main highway and began the drive. I was driving the VW and I think Gunther had the Mercedes.

About four hours into the drive as we were driving across the countryside, Bhante directed us to pull over. We drove off the highway onto a small dirt road. We followed the small road for awhile then turned again into a smaller road or private driveway that had a small lean-to structure on it. No one was around and it seemed either deserted or not being used at the time.

By now it was raining; a misty rain. We hadn't eaten a real meal yet and Bhante wanted the Mercedes rearranged. We had a small propane cooker and we quickly made rice and tea. We ate digestives with jam, rice and some carrots; all from the generous donations of the Myat Shi family.

Once finished eating, Bhante came out of the bus and stood a little apart from us. He instructed us to take out all the contents and place them in groups. Mattresses to one place, food to one place, cooking items, our luggage -- all were separated into categories on the ground.

He walked slowly around each pile and after he had carefully examined the piles, he began to point to one pile then another. We hustled ourselves around each pile and quickly obeyed his rapid instruction; placing items into the van as quickly as he pointed and directed us. It didn't take long to have the van repacked. It was actually a much better layout for us and much more suitable for the long drive. We could all access our luggage and the mattresses were piled on top of each other and side by side so that we could sleep when we were not driving. The cooking area was at the back by the double doors so that we could cook effectively; all we had to do was open the two back doors and a mini kitchen of propane stove, food and water were available to us.

I walked over to Charlotte, who was standing near Gunther and we began to visit. It didn't take long to feel close to Charlotte. We were the only women amongst six males and we began to work together well. Charlotte was an excellent organizer with a good head on her shoulder. We did a lot of the cooking or cleaning. There were other chores as well and those of us that didn't do one thing did another. For instance, I never filled the water jugs or filled the vehicles up with gas on the trip; in all someone was always doing something.

Charlotte's parents were on vacation so she had hurriedly left them a note. She was still wondering if she really had done what she really had done. This was unlike her usually methodical character and she herself seemed to be in a daze by her own actions. Gunther and she had been together for years. She was deeply in love with Gunther but this was a whole new thing just taking off leaving caution to the wind. She had a passport but visas and proper medical records were not quite taken care of. How would this all work out?

Duff was on Bhante's "list" the moment he arrived back at the Myat Shi's. With no proper titles to the cars and there not being quite enough room to seat us comfortably and Bhante kept mentioning "cramming us in like goats".

Whenever we pulled over it seemed that Duff quickly found the nearest café to duck into and we could always track him down there. He knew most of the owners and he would get up to date information of the conditions of the road up ahead. It also kept him clear of Bhante. The rest of us stayed away from the tension and continued on about our business. There was lots to do; cooking, cleaning, packing and repacking.

In truth, he was just the person to get me riled up and challenge my attitude. We butted heads a lot and I was always rolling my eyes whenever he said something and vice versa.

Yes, Duff was larger than life, a true character, but he was also a professional in border crossings and cultural know-how. We crossed borders we shouldn't have thanks to Duff. Yes, we were crammed in and yes, there was that delay in England but there was also his knowledge and questionable practices that guided us safely through some much untamed territory. In all he was a necessary ingredient to our group. I never would have made it to India without him and I will always be grateful for his presence.

Nevertheless, it was comical at times when you would see Bhante and Duff together. This tall Brit and this short elderly Buddhist monk in orange robes; Bhante shaking his fist and a humbled Duff trying to explain things, which only made it worse. No one liked to be on the "bad side" of Bhante, it was just too humiliating. I would learn that the hard way in India. Repeat after me, "The Teacher is always right, the Teacher is always right."

CHAPTER 15

"Oh boy" is all I can say from this point on. We had bounced all over London and a few hundred miles around and about it but this was something bigger; something so much bigger that it could only be measured in present moments of half asleep, half-awake or on-the-clock driving. We were put on a continuous four hours on and four hours off driving shift. Those of us that drove, Duff, William, Gunther and I were to have company when we drove. This buddy system would keep us awake and give us some much needed company. I only drove the VW bus. That made it difficult to talk with anyone for any length of time because Bhante was occupying the back area. There was a curtain between the front and back and we tried to talk quietly but more often than not Bhante would shush us at some point and we would have to gesture and move our lips silently. So you can figure out how effective that was in the middle of the night and no street light illuminating the cab for lip reading.

That, for me, was the hardest part of the drive; the dark of night in unknown territory. At one point Adam, who was my "keep me awake companion" this particular time, mentioned the steep incline and I simply could not see it. I had been driving for hours and I literally could not tell that I was driving *up* a hill. Then there was the "game" of light flashing with the lorries that were coming from the opposite direction. If the truck flashed you it was an invite to play the game. You would flash back and then we would begin the process of driving with lights off while the truck kept his on and back and forth until one of us got nervous and kept their lights on. I, of course, lost every time. But it kept me alert and awake.

Alaskans are used to roughing it. Outdoor toilets and no running water were not new to me. The adjustment wasn't difficult. We used whatever facilities were available to us whenever we stopped for petrol. Traveling from West to East would slowly strip away any and all hesitations I might have held towards using any facility anywhere in the world. Water was water; boil it of course. Toilettes were toilettes where you either sat on a seat or squatted over a hole in the broom closet; one did what one had to do but quickly, please! Oh, and by the way, let me tell you about the toilet paper… Not!

Unless we were buying local veggies or some other food or gassing up, our hurried pace kept us from sightseeing in general. We could not use the Autobahn as hoped for due to that slight problem with the titles on the vehicles so we had to take a route that went eastward just skimming the border of Germany.

We passed countless signs on the highway in both German and French. When I first saw the green highway sign with the word AUSFAHRT on it, I looked around to see if anyone else in the auto had noticed. Aus*fart*? *What the heck was that?* I snickered to myself and recalled a time when I typed a report for my sister. It was about Ancient Egypt and their various modes of transportation. She would get extra credit if it was typed so I volunteered to type it for her. I worked late into the night to get it done in time for her to turn in the next day. I was pretty tired when I finished. A few days later, she came home from school looking angry as heck. In my typing and tiredness I had transposed a word so rather than typing "The Egyptians floated on *rafts* down the Nile", I had typed, "The Egyptians floated on *farts* down the Nile." Her paper had a note from the teacher on the top "watch your spelling" and the word *farts* was circled in one bold stroke from a bright red pen.

The more I tried to get my mind off of the incident one of those AUSFAHRT signs would appear and I would start laughing again. Bhante was sleeping in the back so there I drove, alone, with those sweet sounding French village road signs of Lucerne, gruyere, fleur de this or that and up would jump AUSFAHRT, *mademoiselle from Amsterdam, parlez vous?* **AUSFAHRT, AUSFAHRT!**

Yeah, I know it was childish, but I hadn't slept in almost twenty hours and was feeling just a little too punchy.

I found out later that ausfahrt meant exit ramp in German. *Figures*, I thought to myself. The German language struck me as such a hammer-heavy dialect. French on the other hand was like a symphony of harmonious notes and sweet sounds. The French would surely never float on farts I thought.

The French countryside was pretty with hay fields bordered by nice lines of trees, but as in any major highway we were cutting through the farmlands; avoiding small towns and local scenery. Although we didn't get to tour around as much as I would have liked I found the area pleasant. Whenever we pulled over the French were cordial and polite; I used my four years of high school French once, "Avez vous le toilette?" Then off we went again. I learned in England to use the word toilette, loo or water closet (WC) instead of bathroom.

"A bath *room* is for bathing," I was told. We Americans were so ignorant.

CHAPTER 16

It was nighttime when we hit the Swiss border. It wasn't my shift so I was half asleep and can barely remember entering Switzerland. It didn't take long to get to the Swiss-Austrian border. We waited for the border to open and were told we had to purchase or rent chains for the pass due to the heavy snowing in the higher altitudes. We stopped in Innsbruck to return the rented chains and were granted a small amount of time to be tourists.

Innsbruck was a snow-covered mountain village with picture perfect chalets and shops with beautifully painted wood signs hanging above each establishment's doorway. I went into a sweets shop for chocolate. The tiny jingle of the overhead doorbell and the smell of chocolate brought me into chocolate heaven. There were uncountable packages of chocolates. I stood and turned full circle; taking in the sweet aroma of chocolate and viewing the colorful wrappings that lay on floor to ceiling shelves. Wow! Where to start, where to start? I made a few purchases of chocolates for the trip and had them eaten long before we entered Yugoslavia. But what fun to see Innsbruck right after a fluffy soft snowfall.

As we descended to the lower elevations of Austria we beheld the dark green Alpine forests. We were on a highway but not the same as in France in that we were driving through the local countryside of Austria where trees hung over the small road and cows roamed the hillsides. This must be Bhante's favorite country, I thought to myself -- green everywhere. Castles built on the hillsides would pop out; partially hidden in the verdant forest. The streams were slow and deep; reminding me of the many streams we had in Alaska. Austrian roads were clean and the drivers were courteous and unhurried. I noticed that all the local autos had amber/yellow glare proof headlights which made driving much easier than in other countries. It was a welcome relief to my eye strain. In the seventies when we were driving through, there wasn't the heavy traffic like it has today.

The deep greens and mellow waterways, along with courteous drivers is a velvety-textured memory. Even though our pace was rushed, Austria was tranquil.

Can you remember as a child playing with toy cars on an electric track? The downhill stretch was the toughest because you picked up speed and there was always an element of tension as your little toy car rounded the corner? Bam!

Everything changed when we crossed into Yugoslavia.

Today, as a result of civil war, the country has broken into several socialist republics; in other words there are now several countries where Yugoslavia once was. Driving through Yugoslavia back then was completely different - or maybe not. What a daunting task for me. The traffic was bumper to bumper with beeps and passing along any stretch of the road. Things just whizzed by me as I gripped the steering wheel. I didn't dare look left or right and kept my eyes on the road ahead. What a transition it was to go from the "yodel-ay-hee-hoo" simplicity of the Swiss-Austrian roadways. I was compelled to keep up with the fast moving traffic for fear of being run of the road. It was unexpected chaos and white-knuckle exhausting.

We slowed down to enter into a traffic jam; I could see police cars flashing up ahead. As we came to the site where the police cars were gathered, a policeman was directing traffic around the scene of a deadly car crash. As we passed the accident, I could see several lifeless bodies scattered in a field no more than twenty feet from the road. We could not have been too far behind when the accident occurred because the bodies appeared to be resting right where they had landed, with their arms and legs spread eagle as though in the act of making snow angels. Small handkerchiefs or pieces of cloth covered their lifeless faces. It was a somber moment. Once we passed the scene, it was the hell highway all over again; pick up speed, hold on tight and keep driving I just kept repeating, *God get me through this country. God get me through this country.*

It was dark when we finally pulled off the highway and turned into a semi-lit restaurant parking lot. I quickly got out of the auto to stretch and breathe. I remarked about the awful driving/drivers. What the heck kind of country was this?

"The coastline of Yugoslavia is said to be one of the most beautiful in the world and the roads are said to be some of the worst in the world," Duff remarked.

"Yeah, tell me about it," I said as I groaned and arched my back in a big stretching motion. So, it wasn't just me and my fatigued and edgy nerves playing tricks on me; this road was cruel.

I went into the restaurant area to purchase a few things and then use the toilette and slap some water on my face. The waiter that approached us in the foyer was extremely friendly. His eyes lit up when he learned some of us were from America. He literally followed us into the ladies room and continued to talk about relatives he had in America and how he wanted to immigrate there. It was a bit unsettling that he followed us right in but, thank heavens, there were no lights on in the bathroom. It was pitch-dark and one had to feel the way to the toilettes. I shut the door to the stall and he kept talking the whole time I was in the loo. I came out of the stall and he didn't miss a beat; washed my hands, splashed water on my face and he was still going on and on about America and his dream of being there. If it hadn't been such a bizarre situation in the ladies room, no lights and all, I would have enjoyed the talk. He was a nice young man and you could see his sincerity. I certainly hope he made it to America.

Traffic-wise, I was relieved to get into Bulgaria. When we neared Bulgaria, Duff told me that it was a communist country. I probably knew that, but little bits of local knowledge always helped me notice where we were and get my bearings. The border crossing into a communist country was as I had imagined; somber and lacking color. All the back-home cold war propaganda clouded my vision and I couldn't help but worry about Charlotte and her unplanned visa-lacking passport. No smiles here that was for sure. The drive through Bulgaria lacked energy; almost void of color. As we drove through the small towns, there were no signs of life. The streets were clean and the houses neat but all I saw was brown. It was interesting that this communist country was so lackluster. The only human I remember seeing in the whole country was an elderly lady sweeping her sidewalk. Surely there were others but I can't remember anyone else. No other country held such a stamp of sadness and lack of color.

CHAPTER 17

Turkey was like a memory. I can't tell you in what lifetime I was there, but I *remembered* it. The instant we crossed into Turkey; I felt a surge of energy. Forget Europe, the East livened my spirit and for whatever reason I was instantly at home. What a country; the sounds and sights struck chords deep within my soul. I noticed that I could pass for a citizen of any country after that. We had been driving furiously and what a blessing when Bhante announced that we drivers could actually have a room for the night in the next town. Before this, whenever we were off our shift of driving, we would sleep in the back of the Mercedes van. We had successfully rearranged things in France and it held good throughout the trip. It wasn't always an easy sleep. Sometimes, it felt like being popcorn in a popper with all the bumps and bouncing. A good night's sleep would be just perfect at this point. I don't know the name of the town or the name of the hotel. Duff took care of the bookings; I got a key; it was upstairs and that's all I cared about.

Being the only female driver, Charlotte got to room with me. We went up to the room and checked it out. It was a narrow room with institutional green walls of stucco/plaster with two small beds on each side of a small night stand. I unfolded the covers to see several creepy crawlers under the sheets. I quickly swept them away before Charlotte would see them. "Here you take this one." I told her after discreetly getting the pests out. Incidentally, my children would laugh at this-I am a real *"scaredy" cat* when it comes to insects. I guess I was too tired to feel squeamish.

The shower at the hotel was also the broom closet. So amongst the plungers and mops we were to take our showers. We all took our turns showering and warning each other about something we had noticed in the closet, *hanging light bulb with exposed wires, dirty plungers in left corner, wear your flip flops* and on and on; each one adding a new warning as we passed the key off to the next person in line.

After placing our luggage in the room and showering we went out into the streets. As we came down from the second-floor the activity rose up to greet us. Our vans were parked right outside the hotel and on the street level was an outdoor café which was surrounded by all the sounds of an eastern city's night life. Some of our guys were drinking ouzo with the locals at one of the sidewalk tables. I ordered a salad and was served a bowl of fresh raw vegetables, beans and lettuce saturated in a perfectly seasoned vinaigrette dressing along with a thick slice of heavy, chewy bread. The meal was delicious and after I finished with the salad, I sopped up the remaining dressing with the crusty bread. The bowl was polished clean when I was finished. It was gastronomic bliss. It is still amazing to me how fresh everything was. There was a self-sufficiency that seasoned everything with such vitality. Fresh and raw; toothsome and chewy!

Whew! I was exhausted from all the driving and Charlotte was ready for bed as well so we said our good nights to the gang and climbed the stairs to our second floor room. After we had gotten into our beds and said good night to each other, we turned out the lights. The activity in the street was muffled by the thick plaster and cement walls and all seemed quiet except for the sound of slow, shuffling feet coming up the hotel stairs. The footsteps came up to our level and crossed over to our door. Quietly the person on the other side of the door tried to gain entry into our room. I could hear the handle being turned ever so quietly. I had locked the door but the next thing I knew the footsteps went to the terrace and through the frosted glass windows the silhouette of a large man could be seen. There was a veranda outside of our room, which our window opened out to. It was a large frosted glass double window; the kind that opened out like a double door.

"Charlotte, did you lock the window?"

She whispered back, "Yes."

Once the person realized he could not gain access to our room his silhouette moved away from the window and we heard him walk slowly to the stairwell and descend the steps. When we felt we could turn on the light we did so and Charlotte went down and got Gunther to spend the night with us. It was just another day or night and I was too tired to dwell on what had just happened; I knew we were safe with Gunther. This moment defined Charlotte; she took nothing for granted. Her attention to every detail and careful planning most likely saved us.

For the first time in my life, my fatigue put me into a deep sleep. No sooner had I closed my eyes than Adam's tap at the door startled me from my almost comatose state. I kept saying, "It can't be six hours, it just can't be." It was, and off we went into the beautiful dawn's light in the remote land of Turkey ever heading east.

Later when we talked with each other about what had happened at the hotel I was told that it was probably because of Charlotte being a blonde and how fair-haired women were rare and found to be attractive in the East. I was surprised to learn this but Charlotte was indeed a fair young lady with natural blond hair. It was a bit unsettling to realize we were in a strange land and had to allow for the behaviors of a different way of life.

CHAPTER 18

Istanbul! The city that extended into two continents; where Europe ended and the East began at the Bosporus Strait. The thought that we had come this far and were midway to our destination was uplifting. I had heard the term Euro-Asia but the idea of being heart and soul in Euro-Asia was almost unbelievable for me. It would have been a great place to stretch out and look around but not so for us. Bhante was adamant about our driving time and Istanbul would have to be driven through on the same day we arrived.

We did get to experience the famous Turkish baths though. We would be allowed a small amount of time to bathe. Charlotte and I found a woman's bath house and the men went off in another direction. There were stalls to undress and towels hanging nearby for the taking. We went to our stall, undressed and wrapped the white cotton towel around our mid-sections. We entered into a large room of floor to ceiling; wall to wall white marble all in pristine condition. The women were lounging about on the marble benches that surrounded small "ponds" of steamy water. The air was wet and warm. It was a friendly gathering of groups of women perhaps family or friends carrying on quiet conversations or laughing about one thing or another.

I felt a little modest; I didn't really know how it all worked in the sense of a steam bath in Turkey. In Alaska we had a sauna on the family property and we used it all the time; heat rocks over a 50 gallon drum stove and throw water on it, hiss and sweat. But here, in turkey it was not so small and private. We sat down on the warm marble seats and talked about the trip so far and what lay ahead. I had grown close to Charlotte by now and we shared a lot of personal things with each other; our relationships, our interests, our family and how it all brought us to this present moment. It was good to stop and sit still for a while and just be human.

There were showers to clean off in once we felt we were ready to leave. I had a headache at the time and if I had to do over, I would have stayed longer and just let the warmth sink in more. We met the men outside so it was probably perfect timing for us to end when we did.

Bhante was cheerful in his greeting and asked us if we enjoyed the bath. He had a kerchief over his head and it was almost comical to see him in his orange robes and head-covering among the mostly black clad Turkish citizenry. As we walked to our parked autos, we smiled and talked about how much we had enjoyed ourselves. Duff kept urging me to talk Bhante into staying a night here but I knew it wouldn't work. Oh, how much fun that would have been and I did wish I could change Bhante's mind but this wasn't the moment to test the waters; best to just accept and move on.

We took the ferry across the Strait avoiding heavy traffic on the bridges, leaving. Istanbul a few hours before dark; right at the time the sun spread a beautiful golden web across the city. The minarets of the several noteworthy mosques stood tall amongst the clusters of buildings and houses. What a beautiful city. Where everything seemed brown in Bulgaria, everything here had a touch of gold reflecting outward.

We kept the pace going and skirted around the Sea of Marmara. There were tall condo type structures that faced directly into the Sea. The waves were hitting the shoreline and I could see a few people walking about. I longed to go there and walk around but we passed by and continued on, resuming our manic frenzy of 4 on 4 off.

CHAPTER 19

The next day, as I rounded the corner of a small hill, a Turkish speed trap greeted us. There were at least two policemen there and they flagged us over. Of course I was speeding -- one of them held one of those speed guns as the other approached the bus. I pulled over and he asked for 5 lire and my driving license and passport. He told me to place the money and license in the passport and hand them to him. I did so and for a matter of record, it is the only time I used that International Driver's License I had purchased for fifteen whole dollars from the back of Seventeen Magazine.

He took the documents, opened the passport to where the money lay and took the money out. Slowly he looked up at us and leaned into the bus. I said nothing and Bhante just smiled. Then, as though in slow motion, he leaned out and turned his head downward, placed the money back between the pages, handed the whole lot back to me and wished us a safe journey. That was it. Bhante's smile was magic and I drove off not losing a penny, lire or farthing.

I am certain I don't need to go on and on about the driving getting tiresome. At times like the speeding incident, I would get a little disconnected or lose track. Bhante sat up front with me on many occasions and I was alone with him. In one way it was great;

his presence was always calming but in another way, I had no one to talk to. Consequently, I would "space out" every now and then.

I was still in Turkey clipping along at a good pace behind a lorry that was hauling telephone poles when the second mishap occurred. The poles extended far beyond the back of the truck and there was a red rag tied around the end of perhaps one or two of the poles. We were both entering on to the highway accelerating peaceably, when the lorry either stalled or struggled with shifting gears and abruptly stopped in front of me. I knew there was nothing I could do but stall the VW Bus. (I had to stop the bus so quickly that I knew the brakes wouldn't do. Honestly, I don't know what made me think to stall out) It lurched forward as it stalled and I cringed at the expected collision. The last thing I saw was the poles rapidly coming for our front windshield. In what seemed like the twinkling of an eye I looked up and the lorry was more than twenty feet in front of us entering onto the highway; going its merry way! I turned to Bhante, who was sitting up front; not knowing what to say, I just looked at him.

I was embarrassed and shaken up over what had just taken place. I wanted to turn to him and say, "Wow! What the heck happened back there?" Yet, there was no time to dwell on it. Bhante said nothing and turned his gaze to the highway; I accepted the obvious as incredible as it seemed; it was a small miracle -- we were being watched over or I just gave up one of my nine lives.

This incident jolted me back to something that had happened just a few weeks before leaving for England. I was driving on a small stretch of highway between Anchorage and Palmer. It was evening; my lights were on but it was not entirely dark so that both lanes of autos could easily see one another. There was a straight stretch with a deceptive little curve up front of me and as I approached the slight curve, headlights appeared in my lane coming right at me. It was the same thing, a head-on seemed imminent to the point that I could do nothing. Then it was as though I came out of a slumber and the car was in his lane and moving past me; no collision. I remembered being a little perplexed back then about what had happened. I will never be able to explain either event based on quantum logic but there you have it. So, how many lives had I lost or gained by the time I almost hit the lorry?

With the dawn came shift changing and breakfast. Duff let us know that after breakfast there would be no more water. What do we do when we're in the middle of Turkey and no town in sight? We went about preparing breakfast as we tried to figure something out.

Two shepherd boys who had come on their donkeys to watch us stood by listening. They couldn't have been more than ten to twelve years old. They were dressed in traditional white cotton pajama pants, pullover cotton tops that went down almost to their knees and a short wool jumper/sweater over the top. It wasn't uncommon to attract the locals whenever we pulled over. Small groups might gather around us and look at our license plates, see what we ate and maybe ask for American cigarettes.

After listening to us for a while, one of the boys approached Duff and by pointing and nodding indicated that they knew where water was -- good water; guaranteed-exclamation point! Duff shrugged his shoulders and gave them our two large five gallon jugs. One boy dismounted and tied the jugs to his donkey. The other young man stayed on his donkey and rode away, leading the other donkey with the jugs behind him. The one that stayed behind had a great time watching us. He would move around to get a better view to watch us cook or pack and follow along with our talking; smiling or laughing with us as if he could understand every word. He was a friendly boy and had the essence of a kind spirit.

We made tea with the last of our water. While I drank my tea and began my usual quick-as-you-can sightseeing scan of the area, I noted that we were in a broad valley. The grass was autumn gold with tufts of surviving green mixed in. I could see rock outcroppings on some of the larger hillsides; a few boulders and shards of broken rock lay about at the base of the rocky patches. There weren't any trees around us. It seemed to be the perfect place for sheep to roam and graze, which there were. They dotted the landscape and were spread out either on the hillsides or in the small swales. Not a car passed by this early in the morning; a small breeze was the only sound competing with the silence. Over the caravan hoods I saw a tall mountain. I held my gaze toward the mountain and walked around the autos to get the full view. It was snow covered and stood out from anything else around it. There was not a cloud to be seen and this prominent patriarch, against the back drop of cold blue sky presided over the whole valley. I cradled the hot cup of tea in my hands and contemplated this mountain. It was as though I had walked into a new sphere of influence; not seen or heard, the mountain cast off a high caliber life force; as though tuning in to a particular intangible frequency.

When the shepherd boy returned with the full jugs of water, he motioned for us to drink. His enthusiastic nods and gestures once again assured us the water was safe. Since we didn't drink the local water without boiling, we were a little apprehensive to drink right from the "tap" but as he passed the cup around I took a full drink of the spring water. *What?* The water came alive in my mouth and as I swallowed I felt it moving through my mouth, down my throat and into my stomach. Words cannot describe the life I felt moving through me in the drinking of one small cup of cold, clear water. Was this like it was back in The Garden days when we were so close to God that everything expressed the holiness of life? *Holy water --* the words popped up in my mind and I was startled by the experience. I had drunk from pure mountain streams back in Alaska yet, never had I tasted water that expressed such strength. It was one of those invisible moments, deeply private but silently explosive in my soul.

The boys were happy to see that we were pleased with the water. They hung around with us smiling and nodding and watching us closely. When it came time to leave, we packed up and offered the young shepherds money. No, they did not want any money. Duff gave them some American cigarettes but they were reluctant to take even that. We all piled back in the vans to take our leave. They were smiling and waving good-bye as we entered the roadway.

I had just completed my shift so I was sitting in the Mercedes van passenger side and Duff was driving.

"This is a special place." I remarked, half to myself.

"It's Mount Ararat, you dummy" Duff replied.

"Mount Ararat?"

"Yeah, Mount Ararat; Noah's Ark and all that…"

I nodded slowly but did not speak. As we pulled away and I watched the mountain get smaller and smaller, I tried to remember what I had learned about Noah's Ark. My memory brought back the flood, a bird with an olive branch and vaguely I recalled something about a mountain. I would have to research this when I got home.

Well, I thought to myself, if there really was a Noah's Ark; it surely *was* here.

Duff gave me his *stupid American* look and off we went on our way.

CHAPTER 20

Well, here's the deal with Charlotte and how we handled her rapid exit from England: during our drive, we smuggled her across one border; she hid in the mattresses as we passed through. It was Bulgaria, Turkey or Iran, I can't remember now. Whatever one it was, she hid herself well and we were able to cross without incident. Duff also brought along girlie magazines and American cigarettes for any border guard that needed a little nudging to allow us to pass and he did just that at some of the borders. I was amazed that he knew just what was required at what border. I also helped forge a few medical records for Charlotte's health book that allowed another border crossing, something about certain immunization shots that were required for entry into the country. In all we managed to get through the borders without incident. I do hope the statute of limitations is up on my petty crimes and misdemeanors!

We crossed into Iran and made our way to Tehran. Even though we were rushed, each country left an impression. Iran struck me as the friendliest so far. While we were pulled over at a park a Mercedes sedan pulled up and the driver and two passengers shared their watermelon with us. They asked us where we were from; all the usual questions and welcomed us to Iran.

Then, over walks Ron. He had an amused yet perplexed look on his face.

"They just asked us if we wanted some pot!"

"Are you kidding me? Right, -- no thank you but let me go ask the elderly Buddhist monk sleeping in the back of that VW bus if he'd be interested," I joked.

I leaned a little behind Ron to get a better look at them. They were well dressed professionals and I would never have presumed them to be selling pot. I guess after they knew we weren't looking for pot but Nirvana, they bid us good-bye; we heartily thanked them for sharing their watermelon with us and we headed east.

Iran was a mountainous drive. The steep mountain sides were a mix of trees like ash, elm and firs, etc. Much of the Iranian mountainous region reminded me of the Midwestern United States. A mountain stream ran beside the roadway. We went up and down through the mountains and whenever we came to the bottom of a steep decline the stream would be there; similar to a drive through Montana.

This road in Iran was well maintained. What I was told was that the Shah of Iran received money from the US, which made him wealthy but also produced these elegant highways. It was strange to see roads so well maintained by our dollars and to remember the developing roads in our country. Every country that had received our aid had excellent, well designed road systems. Amazing...

We were in the middle of Ramadan so there were few shops open and much less activity in Tehran. I was disappointed that I wouldn't be able to view a normal street scene in the capital city. I did see a few women covered head to toe walking down a side street though. Just those two walking along, while the rest of the town appeared abandoned or more literally all closed up. Some stray dogs roamed the streets but even they were scarce. We spent only the time it takes to circle through to get on the road pointing us eastward to the Caspian Sea.

Once we were on our way out of Tehran, we came through flat farmlands. Along the roadway we met an old woman pushing a cart full of cabbages. We slowed down and leaned out of the window pointing to her cabbages. She gave us a couple of heads from the cart but would not take any money. I was deeply touched at her generosity.

I looked around and as far as my eye could see there were fields of crops growing in well-tended rows. My thought was that she was probably coming from one of those fields. Was her day ending? I didn't know. She had the look of hard work written in every line of her tanned and tired face. A few dollars would have gone a long way, I was certain, but she opted to give without expectations. This woman would have no tax write off for her charitable act; no one would be aware of her generosity. She simply gave. Her labor in the farmlands produced cabbages and we received them with gratitude. We will never see each other again but I will never forget her sacrifice to share with us. In these small ways we know that there are people all over the world caring and sharing without expectations. I do believe it's a love thing.

While we were eating our meal on the side of the road we talked about getting to the Caspian Sea. It shouldn't take too much time to get there and I was excited at the thought of swimming in salt water. *Would I really float?* I had to find this out. As we drove to the sea, lush green marshlands and tropical vegetation began to emerge. I was seeing a lot of huge homes, all white stucco and wrought iron and half hidden by the rich green, well-tended landscapes.

Had I missed something? It seemed almost instantly that the beautiful mountain forests were replaced by rich green trees, tall grasses and mixed in this were tropical plants of one kind or another. I guessed that the four hour shifts had caused me to miss the gradual change in elevations and subsequent changes to the topical greenery. It seemed we had descended but had we, really? I just didn't know by then.

Tall, marshy grasses surrounded us as we turned off the main thoroughfare onto a small unpaved side road. The smell of damp sand and soggy marshes welcomed us as we bumped along the small sandy road. We came out of the marsh to a nice empty stretch of sandy beach. The Caspian Sea spread out in front of us; it was broad and I could not see any hint of its far end. Our caravan came to a stop and we all got out and got ready for swimming. I dressed down to my underwear, as did the rest, and went in. We actually floated just like I had been told we would in the salty water! We spent at least an hour bouncing around the water and laughing, enjoying the respite from the long drive. During the time we spent there, no other autos came down the road we had taken.

I felt my batteries had been recharged and I was more relaxed as we headed out. The only problem was my hair. I couldn't wait to wash it in the Caspian Sea. I had purchased a bottle of local shampoo at a market; the shampoo had to be shaken up before applying; that should have been my first clue. As I poured it over my head, it didn't lather up as I expected. As I tried to rinse it out, my hair felt like I had glue in it and when it dried I looked like a bad hair day shampoo commercial. As I drove, I kept looking in the rear view mirror at my hair and mentally scolding myself for having to try the local apothecary concoctions. Clean hair would have to wait.

Afghanistan was not too far ahead and off we drove.

CHAPTER 21

Apart from every new country and the new vibes that seemed to accompany each border crossing, Afghanistan had that something extra. Was it from their brightly embroidered and colorful clothing or the ready smiles they shared with us? It seemed a mix of this along with their simply genuine nature; not being based on wealth or power but on an inner life and faith that they practiced as they moved about their daily lives. Smiles radiated from the heart.

On one of the first days into Afghanistan, we pulled over and built a fire. We had purchased some local bread and a few other food staples. Afghani bread was different from a loaf of bread back home; it was flat and boat shaped. We heated it over the campfire by poking sticks into it and holding it above the flame; toasting it just slightly. And-so it was, a little before dark somewhere in Afghanistan, that we gathered around the fire and ate our meal of sultanas, walnuts and the toasted bread; warming ourselves, talking and laughing. It was a warm and tasty welcoming to Afghanistan that evening.

Alaska didn't have many fresh things available when I was growing up. We had The Matanuska Valley in Alaska which produced many cold season vegetables but fruits and nuts were imports from the *lower 48*. I had never eaten much fresh anything, most especially nuts or freshly dried fruits, so my tastes buds were snapping and popping with the excitement of such exotic foodstuffs. "We ate *sultanas* in Afghanistan." Oh yes, that sounded so sophisticated and worldly.

We were *in the zone* at this point. I couldn't tell you how many days it took to get from Dover to Delhi. Our drive and activities, as I said before, were clocked not by miles or days but by moments. Cooking, cleaning, driving, sleeping seemed to gauge our progress and punching in to the time clock of life hovered outside the ball of mystical energy that moved us through the days and the many countries. I like it better that way, don't you? – Just a present moment experience – one right after the other.

One of the many brilliant experiences we were all privileged to have was in the town of Herat, Afghanistan. I'd been hearing about it for some time now. Duff had been going on and on about Herat long before we had reached Afghanistan. It clearly held a special place in his heart. He described the pine trees that lined the main roadways that went in and out of Herat; telling us that an earlier ruler had the forethought to bring in the large pine trees and had developed the area as a true oasis in the stark desert. He considered it one of the most beautiful cities of the East with mosques of stunning spiritual significance.

"Wait till you see the mosque." He had been telling us about an incredibly beautiful mosque that was situated in the center of the old town proper.

As we entered the city via the main roadway I took notice of how the ancient pine trees provided heavenly shade along the smoothly paved road It was a quiet town (still Ramadan, I think), peaceful and clean.

We made our way into the center of the city and found the Blue Mosque. First the men got out and went into the mosque. After they returned, I threw Charlotte's coat over my head for a makeshift head cover and went in alone to the central area or what seemed to be the courtyard. The walls and floor; every inch of space was covered with vibrant blues on white ceramic tiles. The blue design was an intricate weaving of geometric patterns. There was gold Arabic writing higher up on the walls on bigger tiles but the brilliant patterns of blue on white dominated my vision.

I tried to take in as much as I could as I stood there in the center of the courtyard. I was overwhelmed with the awareness of the Divine. I said a prayer but felt that my words/thoughts were inadequate so rather than fumble with what I could not even attempt to venerate properly, I stood silently in the center. Gazing upward to the turquoise spires and brilliant blue sky I felt tremendously small as though being a tiny dot in the infinite universe. The colors were so rich in heavenly hues that they seemed to lift my spirits and defy gravity. I turned and walked back to the waiting autos.

"Didn't I tell you? Didn't I tell you?" asked Duff as I got in the van.

I nodded without speaking.

He was excited to have shared this with us and I was once again moved to silence and wanted to remain there -- in that peaceful zone for as long as I could – keeping the moment alive and active in my spiritual center; silence being ever so important.

Then, off we went out of Herat and into the desert. Time waits for no man and neither would Bhante.

Chapter 22

Man, was I cold! I rolled over and wrapped my sleeping bag tightly around me. The van had come to a stop, which meant time for morning breakfast and shift changes. I just didn't want to get up; I was cold and tired. I moaned a little as I stretched myself out and stepped from the van. We were all fumbling for energy and trying to keep warm. This was the Afghani desert. Off to the East I could see the faint promise of morning as a tiny sliver of mango-charged sunlight skimmed the horizon. *My God!* I thought. My breath at every exhale fogged around me and my fingers felt freeze-dried by an instant searing laser-sharp intensity of heartless frigidity. It was as though I was in a meat locker and nothing I did made me feel any warmer. I huffed and puffed on my fingers and rocked on my feet waiting for that first swill of hot tea.

I dreaded taking care of the usual business of morning potty but knew that there was no getting around it. I crossed the road and sprinted to a small dip in the otherwise flat landscape, did my thing, and raced back; body and spirit neck and neck to the finish line where hot tea waited. I was amazed that an Alaskan would be so thrown off by a cold morning, but I was.

Bhante gathered us all around the VW bus side doors and announced we could each have one tablespoon of brandy to warm us up. He was heavily bundled up in all his usual orange non-possession garments, which included an orange, scratchy, hand-dyed woolen knit cap. He was holding a bottle of Brandy in one hand and in the other hand, a tablespoon. One at a time, we went up to him and waited as he slowly poured the brandy into the spoon, then offered a spoonful to each one us. He smiled at us as we sipped our portion and thanked him. When he was done serving the drink, he retreated back into the bus and we quickly cleaned, packed up and got on our way. Moments on the drive could be brief such as this, but memories of his twinkling eyes and warm smile as he carefully meted out our individual portion remains alive and bright in me. Time has never erased such things. Perhaps stars are memories that keep us from forgetting.

As the sun rose higher, the heat descended; once again the windows were rolled down and it didn't take long for my bones to thaw and life restored. I rested my elbow on the window frame while my other hand held the wheel as I let the warming airstreams hit my face. To my left were the distant Hindu Kush mountains; they leaned back and into the clear turquoise-blue sky that arched over us and touched other distant mountains. At the base of the mountains to my left were clusters of black tents and between us and the tents a small camel caravan was slowly moving across the dry desert. Tribal tents, camel caravans; it was another surreal scene; I felt as though I were in a glass bubble looking down; within and without at the same time.

The black tents were interesting. *Wasn't that a little hot?* I pondered this… I would be roasting inside one of those, but it was explained to me that black was actually a cooler "color" for tents here in the desert. I still had a hard time believing it was cooler but the natives knew best and I never had a chance for a firsthand experience.

We drove up to higher elevations where there were stone houses and flocks of sheep grazing in toast colored pastures. *How far was my eyesight carrying me?* The sweep of land and sky seemed infinite. I had no idea of how much further there was to go; India would be there when we got there. I didn't have a clue about mileage to this place or that and frankly, I didn't care to know.

Drive, Drive, Drive -- Days, weeks; time in general going out the window as the mystical, Eternal Rays of Wisdom's Source moved us closer to our destination.

In the grazing fields, I saw large dogs with the sheep. *What the heck kind of dogs are those?* They were guarding the flocks but I had never seen such huge dogs. They looked like a cross between a St. Bernard and an elephant. Each flock seemed to have at least one and even in the flocks that were a distance away from the road, I spotted at least one of these dinosaur-age throw backs. I was grateful to be in the car and just passing through.

As we ventured through a small village, I let up on the gas pedal. It was a standard village town with weathered huts made of stone or a mix of cement and local resources. I didn't see any women but saw a good number of men and children and probably a chicken or two. They crisscrossed the roadway as they went about their daily activities. Once we had driven through the main village proper and gone through the outskirts, I began to accelerate as I anticipated the long stretch of open road which lay right ahead of me. I exercised my fatigued eyes by rolling them from side to side. I rolled my eyes left then over to my right and my eyeballs locked in on a distant movement. About half a mile off the road I spotted one of those dogs with its herd. Although it wasn't that near I clearly saw that the beast had noticed me. It looked up and over at the VW and in a split second, it began to dash towards us.

Surely, it wouldn't attack the car, I thought to myself. It kept coming and coming gaining in speed as it came nearer. At full force, it lunged right at the passenger side of the VW where Bhante was sitting.

We jerked a little; I heard the shattering of glass and crunching sounds as car and canine met. We had actually been attacked by a dog or that is to say the dog had attacked the car! It was beyond belief for me. Luckily, I did not let my foot off the gas this time and we lurched forward. I was terrified and pondered whether to stop and see if the dog was okay? Then, in a split second I realized if the dog wasn't dead, I didn't want to get out of the car. If it had the fearlessness to attack a car, I stood no chance with a mean-spirited, wounded, massive Afghani sheep dog. And how would the native population greet us if I got out? I had no idea how they would interpret what had occurred. I got the feeling that it wouldn't be a warm reception. "Thank you for killing my dog. Now the wolves will come and destroy the flock and we will starve this winter..."

We slowed down a little as I pondered what to do.

"Don't stop; keep driving." Bhante instructed me.

That's all it took for me to leave that town in the dust. I accelerated and kept a rapid pace away from the village. I didn't give a glance to the rear view mirror to see if the dog was dead or alive or if a crowd was chasing us. As I clutched the wheel I stared straight ahead and got the heck out of there as fast as I could.

Once we were safely away from the town Bhante began to chant in Sanskrit. "I know that this accident was not your fault, but it is necessary to pray for the animal and those affected by this tragedy." He told me.

He prayed out loud for about thirty minutes and I remained silent keeping my eyes on the road, hoping I could just get to Kabul without another incident.

A few hours later we were in Kabul; a large city that lies in a narrow valley of the absolutely beautiful Hindu Kush Mountains. What a welcome site for my eyes; all those buildings and houses, streets crowded with life as vendors carted their wares while children played about. Here began the road that would take us to Pakistan, then India. Not much farther now.

Today, Kabul is known mostly for the war and the Taliban but in 1974 it was still a large city that pulsed with cosmopolitan flavor and a diverse mix of people all intersecting within the buzz of city life.

We went to the old section of Kabul where there were open markets and shops selling everything from fresh produce to clothing. This was the heart and soul of the Afghani citizens. I looked forward to being able to walk among the locals and get a real taste of their life and breathe in the fragrance of the open markets.

Duff knew of a hostel near the old city, so we went there first and settled the VW and van into our camping site. The hostel was a large old house with lots of rooms, verandas and toilet facilities. There was ample land surrounding the house and we were parked in a little niche of small trees that provided some nice shade. The many groups of people boarding for the night here were hippies. Several of our group went off and visited with other travelers – comfortable and universal sort of soirée going on here. The doors to the hostel were open and the verandas had all kinds of activity going on; including the wafting scent of cannabis.

This was also where Bhante would leave us and fly to India. Although Bhante had his mission in India, he was still a Cambodian and carried a Cambodian passport and Pakistan did not have diplomatic relations with Cambodia, which made it dangerous for him to cross through Pakistan. Pakistan was already in a state of civil war and with his country having no diplomatic relations with whatever government might be in power made it impossible for him to consider making the drive with us.

We would be taking the Mercedes van to run around in and one of the first stops was the post office where I mailed letters. It was the first time I had written since we began the drive and I wanted family and friends to know that we had made it to Kabul. When I returned to Alaska many months later my father would tell me that when he hugged me and said good-bye that September of 74, he thought it was the last time he would see me alive. I was surprised; I had no idea he was concerned in the least. "Fools rush in..." they say. Thank heavens I was a fool.

As Duff arranged for Bhante's air travel and Gunther went to purchase the parts for repairing the headlight to the VW bus, Charlotte and I hung back at the campsite. Charlotte found some cord to stretch between two trees and we were able to wash and dry some of our clothing. The heat quickly dried everything and it seemed that by the time the clothes were dried, Duff and Gunther had returned.

Gunther began to work on fixing the bus and Duff took Bhante to the airport. Alone at last! No Bhante! We didn't mind his being with us and we knew we couldn't delay much, but we kind of mentally stretched out a little as we took to the streets of Kabul. We wanted to look around at all the shops and get a feel for the city. Since Gunther was repairing the bus, Charlotte and I went together. First we found Duff at his friend's rug shop. We found him sitting on a small stack of beautifully woven eastern rugs drinking tea and smoking with his friend. We let him know our plans and to set a time to meet up with him to return to the campsite.

Kabul was a maze of different shops and bazaars -- Each shop had a particular ware to sell and there were racks of clothing out on the sidewalks for viewing.

Running in and out and back and forth were the young chai wallahs. They carried hot tea in thick tall glasses to the various vendors and their clients. They were the needle and thread of the market community with their scurrying about from shop to shop, connecting us all together. You could hear the glasses of hot tea clanking in their metal baskets while they ran to and fro as the vendors shouted out for their services.

I fell in love with the bright colorful dresses of embroidered bodices and mirrors. I selected one that I wanted and looked for the proprietor of the shop. He was out on the street haggling with another customer and when I got his attention he acted as though I had disturbed him. He came over to me with a sour look on his face, waving his hands and grumbling.

Ok, haggling lesson number one -- always dicker about the price. I asked him the cost of the dress and he said something like 300 Afghanis. I could not haggle worth a darn. I pondered the price and said something else. Then the vendor said something and I said something back, he made all kinds of gestures of despair and disgust and I got it for 150 Afghani dollars or cents -- I never was quite sure about currency. I wasn't certain that I offended him because I was clearly an amateur haggler or if I got a good deal. I didn't care; I loved the dress.

We made our way to a small bazaar that sold burkas as well as other goods and for the first time I was able to have a close up view of women covered in their burkas. I noticed pretty patent leather shoes on one of the ladies feet. There was mesh netting covering the mouth area and I wondered how they could possibly stand the heat.

I think you must know by now that heat was a major concern for me. It was a new thing to be living in a hot climate and with no disrespect intended, I had a hard time imagining how black tents and the shroud of heavy burkas was at all conducive to just plain everyday living. I was getting acclimated as we went further east but would I ever be a hot weather person? Doubtful...

Charlotte and I set about looking for a wedding dress. Bhante had let it be known that no couples would be allowed to live together on the mission. Charlotte and Gunther had come together so it was assumed they would either live apart or marry before the course started. We found a beautiful white cotton dress that was mid-calf in length. This dress also had lovely embroidering but no mirrors and slightly more sophisticated with rich green, red and blue flowered embroidery. It was a perfect wedding dress. She did her haggling and purchased the dress.

Next, we went to a jewelers shop for rings. As we entered the store a local customer was quibbling over a silver ring with the owner. The vendor had offered it for X amount and the local left without trying to work the price down any further. Charlotte liked the ring, it fit and seeing how the price was X when we arrived, Charlotte got it for that good price offered only to locals. We were at the right place at the right time.

My first impression at the border only intensified as my fondness for the Afghani people grew with every heartbeat of time spent there. They were indeed the most hospitable of all the countries -- east or west; in some ways the unpretentious nature of their lives reminded me of the Alaskan natives. The further East we drove the closer I felt to home.

Bhante, now safely placed on a plane to Delhi, we spent the night at the hostel campsite and after a good rest we rose early to begin the last leg of our drive. We were able to get to the marketplace super early to get something hot for breakfast; before the shops would open and the hustle-bustle of shoppers would be crowding the streets.

It was an altogether different scene that greeted me early in the morning. The streets were quiet. I saw wooden beds with no mattresses; heavy ropes woven together and knotted were what kept the frame together and what the owners slept upon. I saw many of these beds lining the vendor areas. *This is where they sleep.* I thought to myself. It was a revelation of the hard work and little rest that the vendor endures. In that brief observation of early morning in Kabul, I was touched by their minimalism. The beds would be put away somewhere before the wares were brought out and the shoppers arrived to begin another day of price negotiations. I felt privileged to see what struck me as the heart and soul of Kabul life before you could apply the makeup or serve the tea.

It was good-bye to Kabul for me. I swept my glance across the city then turned my head up to the Hindu Kush Mountains; one last look: Dawn in Kabul; clear blue sky, crisp and cold with golden threads of morning sun tapping every nook and cranny of this beautiful city. Afghanistan! God/Allah help them, it was a lovely place in 1974.

CHAPTER 23

We reached the border between Afghanistan and Pakistan before sunset but too late to travel through the Khyber Pass. Day drives were only being allowed through the pass. The pass was governed by Pakistan but controlled by the local clans or tribes. I was told that only a few days prior to our arrival, a group had attempted to drive the pass at night -- this proved fatal. Their car had broken down in the Pass; they were robbed and their throats slit.

We were given a space in line with other caravans traveling east, which formed a semi-circle of vehicles in the back area of the border crossing station. Our group was given space in front of a steep hillside.

Charlotte and I took to roaming. There were motor homes, sedan cars, trucks and Lorries all clustered in the little area. Everyone had a story here; goods to be delivered, relatives to see, serious seekers or general tourists; our commonality was adventure. Duff went to the local truck stop area to hang out and we could see him smoking and visiting with the locals as we passed by the one-story building that sold chai.

It was dusk by the time we completed our walk. Campfires were now burning at each parked group. Night was approaching; the small groups of travelers were beginning to close up for the night and were returning to their campsites. At each group there was a sentry posted. Each guard had double bandoleers loaded with bullets crisscrossing their chests.

"The bandits have been coming down from the mountains; slitting throats and robbing the tourist caravans," Adam told me. I stared at the sentry assigned to us; he was genial but kept his distance; sitting on his cot, his rifle propped on his knee, remaining alert and vigilant.

I wasn't afraid in the least, it sounded romantic and in full character of the surrounding history and population; tribes, territories and raw survival. I took little concern. Romantic... I'm being honest. I was certain India was my destiny and I knew I would get there. It was one of those times in my life that the certainty of being where I should be outweighed any apprehension. There were times of feeling vulnerable to the different cultures and their actions but gripping fear? No, not really. I was in awe of the total experience.

The next morning was the Khyber Pass. We took our place in line and passed through customs. Cars were already coming out of the Pass from the east. I would watch one car after another pull over; out came the driver and many passengers crammed into an old American four-door sedan. One of the passengers got out and went to the trunk and opened it to let out, what appeared to be the same amount of passengers from the back trunk! I was blown away. How did they all fit in and not suffocate? It was not a one car phenomenon either, there were several cars doing this and it appeared to be a routine event to get from point A to point B.

There were brightly decorated buses full to capacity with passengers, animals and furniture with some passengers sitting on the roofs or hanging on to the back of the bus. The buses and Lorries of the east were works of art. They were painted in brilliant colors; blues, red, gold, etc. There were tassels of golden rope and beads dangling from the front windows and I could hear music coming from somewhere. The music was different here with voices that seemed to weep and chant at the same time, accompanied by thumping base, twanging stringed instruments and snake-charming wood winds. It was a mix as diverse as the traffic. Shops selling whatever fare were open now for business; I could feel the rhythm of a new day beginning. It was dusty from all the comings and goings and the free-range fowl scratched the hardened dry earth.

The Khyber Pass drive was a little over thirty miles long. Back then it was called the Hippie Trail because of its connection to the Eastern mystical centers that so many of us were traveling from; or going to. Even today, the pass remains a vital trade route between countries and it has seen countless invasions. The rich history coupled with the most recent activity of bandits put me on alert and sharpened my senses to take in as much as I could as we went around and around sharp turns; climbing up then leveling off, and then descending. Slowly and steadily we made our way through the Pass.

The earth around the roadway had a blackened appearance as though thick heavy tar had been poured, spread, and had now hardened over the rocky surface. Beyond the immediate roadway it was barren and dry. What little vegetation there was, it seemed stunted and twisted; with little green foliage.

There was a path beside the road; perhaps down and over just a little but near enough to where I could view the travelers with their mule packs. *Are these bandits?* They stopped and waved up to us as we went by. I gave a small wave and moved my hand to my throat. Their faces were friendly but their bandoleers and guns made me wonder if they were friends or foes. They were dressed in cotton muslin made dirty by the dust and heat. *Could these honestly be bandits that slit throats at night?* We didn't stop to find out, but they struck me as such a contrast to the stories of ruthless bandits that I had heard the night before.

In several areas of the pass as we came upon low flat lands there were fortressed communities. I viewed no signs of life in the wide barren area that lay around them. They were crude fortifications with jagged rock spires at the top that blended in with the parched landscape. Cloth, Doll-like figures, with heads but no faces hung from the rocky serrated edges. *What am I looking at?* I couldn't tell if these were abandoned forts or present day communities. Obviously the hanging figures were to ward off something evil; either present day or long ago. *What is life like in these places?* The slow cadence of driving through such a foreign lifestyle with all its portents and charms made me feel remote and pensive. I was truly a stranger in a strange land.

When we finally made it through the pass and had traveled a good distance, I told William that I didn't think I could drive through Pakistan. Just sitting up front while William drove I observed that this was by far the worst driving conditions I had ever experienced.

The temperament of the road was as broken up as the citizenry. No signs, no pavement; just dark bumpy driving with surprises at every turn. Obviously our foreign aid package was not at work here. One could be driving at a good speed when large boulders, placed haphazardly ahead in the road, appeared as if out of nowhere. It was the Pakistani equivalent of flares for warning drivers of a broken down vehicle or some other hazard up ahead. Swerving back and forth and not knowing what was around the next curve made me uneasy about continuing as a driver. The roads were now "backwards" for me in that we would need to drive on the "other" side of the road. I wasn't at all confident that I would remember which side was which if I had to constantly dodge boulders. I just couldn't get past the fear of forgetting for one minute which lane was which. I had to resign my post of the only female driver of our long drive to India.

That night we pulled over to a roadside inn. The lights were out at the inn and we were the only vehicles around but Duff knew the proprietor. We would stop here for tea while Duff visited with his friend to find out what lay ahead for us. We visited with one another for a little bit as Duff and the owner talked in hushed tones. Once they finished talking, we stretched one more time and climbed back in the vans. Onward we drove, we were getting close to India and time was important.

CHAPTER 24

In less than twenty-four hours from the Pakistani border it hit me... My bowels were twisting and turning and I was nauseous; my head was throbbing with pain and I felt feverish. Without caring where we were, I yelled to whoever was driving to stop.

We stopped near a field that was bordered by large trees and I stumbled down a small trench that followed along the shady border. I tried to get as far away from the group as possible for some privacy. After finding a small area that I felt could somewhat conceal me, almost not making it in squatting position; my bowels purged. I got up and immediately heaved ho the contents of whatever remained in my stomach. With the world spinning and lurching, I made my way back to the car.

At this point I had lost all inhibitions. Whatever decorum I had held on to in the drive went out the window. I don't know how many times we needed to pull over but it seemed every half hour if not more. I lay in the back of the VW sweating and chilled, all at the same time. It was really horrific. My head was splitting and nothing eased the pain. All we had as any sort of medicine was Bach's Rescue Remedy and it didn't do the trick. The heat was on us now and it seemed we would never get there – to India.

As I lay in the bus, I remembered when we had visited with the border guards. *It had to have been that amaroot or whatever it was*. It was the only thing we ate that was out of our ordinary diet. I couldn't quite make out the name of the fruit. The guard had said something that sounded like amaroot as he passed us each a slice. I smiled and nodded a thank you as I received the fruit into my hand. I ate the slice of fruit and blinked at the flavor; it was not sweet or pungent; bittersweet and crunchy-perhaps unripe. The border guards had spoken amongst themselves and one guard mumbled something to the others, which they all found humorous. The English translation was probably something like, "Boy will they have the shits after this"

I mumbled my thoughts, "It was that fruit they gave us." But by this point, who really cared what it was?

After that I didn't see much of Pakistan other than ditches or sides of the road. I stayed in the back of the VW covered up and aching. We finally made it to India and the first town was Amritsar. I was too sick to get up and move around; only peeking out the bus windows. There were quite a few children mulling about the parking area. The girls struck me as being exceptionally beautiful with their dark soulful brown eyes, light chocolate skin and colorful saris; they stood out against the poverty of the dusty brown village. Our drive was almost over. I fell back down and went to sleep.

The honking of horns began almost immediately once we crossed into India. It was necessary to honk through the traffic of pedestrians walking, buses or cars darting here and there and various animals such as the sacred cow, elephant and mule drawn carts, etc.; all were using the road as their private walkway. The beeping was endless and echoed into the night as we drove closer to our destination. I had never seen so many people and heard so much noise. I slept fitfully; being awakened by my illness, bright lights, or when the horn gave an extra-long bleat as our vans swerved in and out of traffic.

Chapter 25

We arrived at the gated archway of the Vihara, a little before dawn. The gate was locked so we rested in the vans while Duff managed to wiggle through the gates and get inside the mission. He came back a little later with the grounds farmer, Siraj. Siraj unlocked the gates and waved us in.

We started the engines and crossed under the archway that announced the Ashoka Mission Vihara. We slowly drove into the complex, road-weary, tired and hungry. We had completed the drive in record time but all felt the fatigue of such a strenuous effort. I was exhausted from being sick and not being able to keep anything down; feeling like I was still hovering somewhere between England and the Mission and the drivers had driven almost twenty hours without sleep. It would take a while for all of us to get grounded and see where we were.

Bhante was glad that we had arrived so quickly but showed concern when he heard that some of us were sick. There wasn't much to be done for us. Eating safe food and time would allow the illness to purge itself from our bodies.

We parked the vehicles and piled out of the cars; yawning, stretching and slowly stepping about. Duff took a few of us into the kitchen area where we were introduced to his girlfriend, Aime. She and a visitor to the mission were hard at work preparing breakfast for us. We said our hellos and let them get on with the cooking.

Aime would be on the course with us. She was a real French beauty; slender with long amber honey colored hair, green eyes, glossy tanned skin. She was wearing a turquoise cotton top with a turquoise skirt. Her eyes were welcoming and friendly as she greeted us. It was an instant kinship. *How can she be Duff's girlfriend?* I thought to myself.

There was a free-flowing connection between so many of us back then. It was like a recognition that was deeper than the surface; a "Hello old friend, long time no see" reunion was going on even at first meetings with each other.

We busied ourselves instantly. There were mattresses to unpack and the leftover food had to be delivered to the kitchen while some worked on breakfast. I was taken to my new quarters by Duff. We walked down the broad common walkway to the first green door on the left. He opened the door and I entered into the ladies dorm, which were two rooms. My room was the back one so I had to come in the front door and walk through the front room to get to my area.

I took my belongings in and rolled out the sleeping bag on my new mattress. If I had not been given a mattress, my bed would have been a nicely made wooden bed; in other words, I would have been sleeping on wooden planks. I looked at the bed and mattress and thought about London and that young man who was so helpless against Bhante's negotiating skills. I smiled and said a silent prayer of thanks. Bhante got the mattresses for *damn cheap* and I was *damn happy* about it. I dropped my gear on the floor and plopped myself down on the bed. The mattress felt great. With my sleeping bag already rolled out I was quite at home. It was enough for me, considering the months of gypsy-wagon lifestyle I had been enduring.

Breakfast was ready in no time and we all gathered around in the dining area and ate our first official standard Indian meal of chapattis with oatmeal (from the trip) and hot tea. The chapatti is made of whole wheat flour and water, rolled out like a tortilla and toasted in a rounded pan. It (the chapatti) is the equivalent to a whole wheat tortilla in America. There was still quite a bit of jam and sugar left over from the drive to supplement the otherwise meager meal, so we ate quite well that morning. It was a delight to sit around and eat knowing we didn't have to rush off over the horizon or into the sunset. We were home.

After the breakfast, I went back to my room and looked around to see where I would unpack the few things I brought along with me. My room was square shaped with a window of two green wooden shutters right in the middle of the back wall. There was no glass in the window. By opening the shutters, I could look out to the back gardens of the mission; mostly farmland with large trees separating several plots of tilled soil. Just beyond there was the back wall portion of walls that enclosed the mission property. A path ran behind the length of the continuous one-story structure of dorms and kitchen/dining area. The path was narrow and maintained only by constant use.

My bedroom walls were white and bare of any pictures. I would have to hammer a few nails in the wall to hang clothes and there was a piece of furniture about three feet in length against the front wall; a dresser/cupboard of sorts. It had two shelves about two feet long and a tiny enclosed cupboard that made up the rest of the cabinet. In all it was about three and half feet long. I folded my clothes and put them on the shelves and placed pens, paper and aerogrammes inside the cupboard. It was a snug little set up. It took all of five minutes to unpack and inspect the layout so I decided to lie down and rest for a while. What comfort, my own bed, my own room; the horns and the honking, the wheels turning and turning, the awful diarrhea and fatigue; my mind went blank and I fell to sleep.

Chapter 26

I awoke, stretched a little and went to take a look outside. I opened the door and sat down on the front doorstep. A little later, Charlotte came out of her room and sat next to me. We were still not up to par but felt so much better just by being here. We were mulling over our long drive and all the things that had happened when Aime came by and asked if we would be eating with everyone else for lunch. I replied in the affirmative and shortly we were called to eat.

Aime had made a dish of pumpkins and garlic sautéed in mustard oil for lunch along with the standard basmati rice. What a taste treat. I had only eaten pumpkins in pies before this and I couldn't get over the wonderful taste of a pumpkin with garlic. It was not too sweet and with a little salt or soy sauce it was a great meal. They had been cut into small thin slices and sautéed until they were el dente; not soft and not crunchy.

With lunch over, I went to help clean up and thank Aime for the great meal. Through the dining area, where we had just eaten, then turning to the right was a small galley type cooking area with gas burners and counter space for food prep. I helped tidy up there and Aime told me where to take the dirty dishes, which was through the galley then left through another long kitchen/storage area. Here we put away any leftover food into the screened cooler for future use and to hang cleaned pots and pans on the wall pegs. The dishes and utensils were placed in open cupboards above the cooler area. The second kitchen area was about ten feet long. I walked out the back door of the second kitchen to the outdoors where the sink and wood cook stove, or fire pit as it was called, were located. Several of us cleaned up under the green tarp that was strung over the fire pits and the kitchen sink. It provided cool shading for us while we finished with the dishes.

After lunch cleanup I went back to the stoop, too tired to move from the steps. I sat there gazing mindlessly into the path watching feet moving back and forth; not feeling at all interested in looking up. In my trance-like state I caught movement out of the corner of my right eye. I observed a tall, skinny Indian in a brown bellhop uniform. The uniform was a good two to three inches too short at the ankles and arms and he had the knobbliest ankles and wrists I had ever seen. He had a bushy, white-as-snow mustache, his skin was dark brown and a dirty turban covered his head making his skinny body appear top-heavy. He looked like a character from a Tim Burton movie. From this small distance I could see he was elderly; weathered and walked wearily.

Who is that? I lifted my gaze and discreetly stared at his movements. He was doing a sort of walking/shuffling over to the spigot, which was across the walk and over to the right of me. As he walked he was mumbling and looking down at the ground. At the spigot, he filled an old tin can with water. In his other hand he held an Indian-styled broom; a thick bundle of tall feathery grasses. About three inches from the top of the broom were bright colorful cords that tightly held the grasses together. Once he had filled the tin, he moved onto the walkway and stooping down just a little, he sprinkled the area with water; he then took the broom and swept the watered-down area. *Oh, I get it*; he was sweeping the area of loose gravel, leaves and anything else that had come to rest on the hardened surface. The process removed the loose upper crust of debris leaving a nice clean dust-proof pathway.

Then I noticed that as each of our group passed by him he quickly, without being noticed, swung the can in such a way to splash water at their heels. When they turned to see what had just hit them he had already turned away, sweeping another area of the ground; acting as though he had nothing to do with whatever just happened to them. He continued to do this with every new arrival that passed him. And if they came by three times they got doused three times. It was interesting to watch as he tested the attitude of each one and then quickly turn and pretend to be sweeping in another direction. If someone looked over at him he would shuffle and mumble away as though he were just a humble sweeper doing his job. They were all being closely observed by him as he mischievously darted back and forth, muttering and acting the idiot. He was taking in their every reaction, which varied from a questioning glance to a sneer of irritation.

He continued to do this for a while until he looked over and saw that I was watching him. He acted startled to see me sitting there. I smiled at him; wagging my finger and shaking my head. He gave me a huge grin and his eyes twinkled with mischievous delight. Shaking his wobbly head and moving away, he continued to sweep the ground.

This was my first encounter with Paagal, the mission's sweeper. That's the kind of person he was; full of mischief and mockery. He delighted in teasing us and as the course went on and on, he was comic relief against the backdrop of intensive meditative effort.

Paagal, which I was told means *crazy* in Hindi, belonged to the lowest caste in India. He was a sweeper of the untouchable caste. Although the caste system has been declared unconstitutional in India, it still remains active in many rural areas. Here on the mission he had his own level of power and he loved to toss it about. Bhante let him come and go and I never saw them interact except once when Bhante gave him some money.

Paagal always dramatized a situation; if he was offended, he shrugged and huffed and mumbled as he walked away. Everything he did was done with flare as though he still lived in the innocence of his childhood. We were all marked by the time the walkway was swept that day and accordingly throughout our tenure he used it to exploit our shortcomings.

CHAPTER 27

Later that day as I went back and forth to the vans for unpacking, I took some time to take a look around. All along, since I had met Duff I had wondered what the mission looked like. Whenever I asked Duff about the mission while we were on the drive, he would just say, "Wait and see. You won't believe it; you won't believe it." Now, as I sat on the stoop I could not believe it.

Although I knew this would be my home for a while, I still felt the distance between the van and my room was all I could claim as familiar territory. The vans had been parked in front and off to the left side of the temple. From the vantage point of the van, I stepped out just a little into the driveway and scanned the layout. The property was a rectangle shaped, twelve acre piece of land with the temple and the adjoining buildings sitting at the back. The Buddhist temple was large and painted a soft rose-pink/coral shade. Its large terrace was about ten or more feet long and spanned the whole of the building. Two sets of steps ran up to the terrace. The main steps, in the center were used by guests and the side steps were used by the residents. The center steps were flanked by some beautiful light magenta and pale white flowered crepe myrtle-type trees.

The mission is surrounded by high stone/cement walls and there are two entrances into the mission; the one we drove through and the foot path at the other end of the property. Both points of entry are locked at night. Just down the driveway, there's a hostel with a chai shop and small cooking area. The structure dates back to the Mogul rulers. It's a beautiful old structure with ornate carvings cut into the red sandstone walls and arches around the windows and doorway.

The hostel is busy with guests coming and going. There is even a motor home parked outside, but they all remain over there by the hostel and do not venture to our area. A Frenchman and his young Indian bride were managing the hostel when we arrived. He was a chef and made the best French toast I have ever eaten in my life. The secret, I was told by him, is to soak the dry bread in a batter over night. Unfortunately they are leaving for France soon.

As I took in the whole scene, I watched Gambhiro, a monk, come out of the temple, slip on his sandals and go down the side steps. Quite a few sandals are gathered outside the temple entrance and one man was receiving a color treatment to one side of the veranda. The patient was a local and I was told that he has TB.

Gambhiro, who will also be attending the course, is the right hand of the mission. He was in charge of managing all the activities for the monastery and any day to day responsibilities Bhante assigned to him. It is hard to describe him because his shaved head and orange robes block me from noticing the individual. He was British and ordained a couple of years before. He was kind and intelligent and always possessed a most genuine smile.

In front of me and between the hostel and our dorms is a patchwork of verdant garden plots. Wherever possible the acreage was being used for food production. Bhante has managed to rummage and scavenge a number of seeds or cuttings that have been left behind by travelers. For instance, the abundant garlic growing in one of the plots was the product of abandoned cloves of garlic a few seasons back. There is also cauliflower, eggplant, cabbage and a number of other items being grown in the varying squares and rectangles of the ziggedy-zaggedy network. There are three or four mandarin trees in front of the patches, a kumquat tree or two, and other undefined shrubs or trees.

The canals that carry and conserve precious water surround the lowered growing beds. All runoff water irrigates one field or another at various times of the day, month or year. Saraj, the gardener, and his family maintain the gardens and by my assessment they have done a wonderful job. Whatever is grown in those fields will be our meals for the next four months. To get to another area on the mission, we would walk through the gardens on the raised pathways.

On a small hill next to the side wall, Saraj, the gardener and his son and daughter-in-law live. It is considered a nice hut for the area and since they live on a small rise of land, they have privacy. The well, directly in front of their house, served as the laundry and bathing area as well as irrigation to the garden plots. A few other crops, carrots, cabbage, onions and probably more cauliflower; all in various stages of development face the well. This small growing area is behind the temple and dorms. There were a few more big trees as well and the back wall was just beyond the gardens. So, basically, we are at one end of the mission and most of the property spreads out in front of us.

I had done enough for the day and as I returned to the dorms, along the front promenade, Guinea fowl were prancing about pecking at invisible objects. There was also a rooster, a pair of ducks, and a white rabbit named Bal de Neige hopping about amidst all the new activity. We also had two stray dogs. Their names were Cookie and Blackie; they guard the mission and eat all our scraps. They are in good shape -- not the standard rabid strays that roam the farmlands. Later, another black dog came to camp with us. He was a small black dog; pointed nose and a curled up tail. We called him a number of names such as Shadow or Lazarus.

The Bodhi tree is down a path to the side of the kumquat trees. It is said that The Buddha received Enlightenment while sitting under a Bodhi tree. This lush green full-bodied tree has a special place on the property. There is a wide path circling around its large trunk and beyond the Bodhi tree are the rest of the gardens and an archway on the left wall that leads to other farmlands, huts, and beyond that; one mile away was a small town. There is a gate at the archway and as I said before, it is locked every night.

All our living and eating area is attached to the temple. Next to the temple is the dining area, then the guest quarters where a former governor and his family from Cambodia are living. In passing, we smile and wave to each other.

Next, the tool shed with all kinds of things inside. Whitewash, hammers, rakes, saws, bits of this and that. Paul from Australia is coming out with a hammer and saw; he almost runs into me. He is full of energy as he goes by – obviously, he was not on the drive. Then there are the ladies, the men's and the couple's dorms. All are the same in size with the same pass through set up; two rooms each.

There's a lot of activity going on. The mission was a true representation of who Bhante was; majestic simplicity in all the shapes and forms, flora and fauna. There are no noisy conversations going on. No horns blaring from fast driving cars to defy the vivid life force that bathes the mission. All life is one here and there is a synchronicity of purpose. I was on the outside looking in at that moment; road weary, ill and tired, but soon the Vihara would sweep me into its current and carry me on my mystical journey.

The unpacking and general lazing about filled the first day. Of course, I quickly made acquaintance with the latrine. The latrines, also dating back to the Mogul days were used by all residents at the mission. It was a long red sandstone building with no roof that was part of the far wall for the mission. There is a women's side and a men's side. No booths for privacy, no running water; just quite a few holes in the raised brick. In the east no one sits on toilettes and here in this outhouse setup it was typical to eastern culture. You would step up onto the raised platform and squat over the hole.

The drop down seemed pretty far and was I surprised one time to see a mongoose staring back up at me. I chose another hole that day. Ah well, one gets used to such things. No toilette paper either. A brass bowl for water and a rag was the standard. The pot could be purchased in any market place. The rags were washed after every using and placed to dry and disinfect in the hot sun. Water was made available at the entrance of the latrines in large buckets with ladles that were kept full by the sweeper for the mission.

The first evening was a quiet one for us. Many of us ate and settled into our rooms after a light evening meal-probably soup. In just that short time at the mission I was recovering from my diarrhea and exhaustion was taking its place. Time for bed and a good night's sleep…

CHAPTER 28

Within the first few days of our arrival, a few of us decided to walk into the nearby town for a few supplies. I went looking for Charlotte to see if she wanted to come with us. I found her in the temple typing Sanskrit prayers into English pronunciations for our use during the course. She was seated in a chair behind an old manual typewriter, which was on an old secretary table. *And where the heck did that come from?* Bhante seemed able to produce anything at just the right moment.

There were copious amounts of carbon paper collated with sheets of paper. She had to press hard on the keys to have the translation copy through onto the many layers of paper and carbon. Today, it would look totally primitive and back then it still looked primitive. She plunked away on the keys for hours. No, she wouldn't be able to come with us.

As she and I visited a little, I noticed the inner temple, which was a large open area with thin carpets spread on the cement floor of the central region where the sitting meditation took place. It was a comfortable place, unlike a western church with wooden pews that have always made me restless. I was at ease instantly in the temple. So much so that I didn't gawk or stare at anything. It was just so natural to be there that my looking was almost lazy and failed to take in much except the serene, relaxing tone it manifested.

A few cushions were set up against the arched columns that ran through the middle of the building. If you were lucky enough to get there first, the columns could provide additional back support. The walls were painted a nice leafy green and the recessed altar for Lord Buddha was to the back wall. There were bright colors, incense pots and smaller statues all neatly set in the shrine area.

It was quiet inside but there was still quite a bit of activity going on in the temple. To the left of the temple doors was where the color therapy was administered. There were several mats available to lie upon and several 150 watt colored lights attached to tripods stood at the ready. The colored lights radiated their healing force down onto the recipient lying on the mat during a color therapy session.

I told Charlotte we'd be sure to go another day before the course began and quickly left the temple to meet up with the group that was waiting for me. The mile-long walk was a pleasant one. Along the path we passed a few people; some locals and some like us who were living at the mission. "Namaste, Namaste", palms together and nodding casually, was exchanged by all as we passed each other. Namaste; the standard expression of hello or good-bye is shared between all people in India. I just loved learning all these things and the first time I used it on the path was a thrill to me. *I'm in India, I'm in India!*

The first part of the walk, as we passed through the back gateway, took us through a field of dry grass and thorny bushes. Walking further took us into the farmlands where the path became elevated above the rows and squares of crops. At one point we walked right through the front yard of a hut where a lady was cooking chapattis on the outside fire pit. Not much later, another hut with a woman refinishing her small outdoor area with a mixture of ashes and dung. After it dried, it would become a smooth and sturdy floor. Namaste to all...

Within twenty minutes we made our way up a small side street of huts and vendor stalls. As we entered into the main street, I was startled to find the scene oddly familiar. It was reminiscent of dreams that I had when I was just a child. When I woke from the dreams I always felt unsettled. The people and structures in the dream were alien to me and although they were not nightmares, they were disturbing.

Now, here in front of me, the dreams of my childhood were being played out-*live*. I recalled the grayness of my dreams as I observed canals of gray water running beside a gray main road. The gray waterway was the color of sludge and run off from the town's many houses and shops. There was no sewage system in the town and I quickly learned where the term "gray water" came from. The odor that roamed the village was new to me though; a homogenized collection of elimination and garbage.

The strange people of dreams past were simply Indians in their saris and local dress of pajama pants, long cotton shirts. The white, sacred cow ambled along the main thoroughfare, eating cast offs from the local vendors. Now I could plainly see that the houses with large garage doors of my dreams were the shops that opened directly to the main street. The garage door or pull-down was how the shops closed up at night. There were no tiny little doors with bells that jingled when you entered the store. The whole side of the store opened to the street. It was all explained or revealed to me in an instant as the memory of my dreams and the village activity merged to another present moment experience.

"Déjà vu" said Ron.

I couldn't quite agree with that because these were recurring dreams and I instantly remembered them when I entered the village. It wasn't a vague something or other. I am not sure I fully understand the concept of déjà vu so perhaps this was indeed déjà vu in its fullest and most viable sense. It took a moment to get my mind adjusted before we turned left down the main street looking at all the wares. If we had turned right we would have followed along more vendor shops and eventually made it to the bus stop.

Shortly along the road something to my right caught my eye and I turned just a little to see what was happening. One of the shops was stacked, floor to ceiling, with mysterious brown loaves of undefined foodstuffs. They looked like loaves of brown French bread, but in looking closer I could see it wasn't bread. The shopkeeper had a pump action bug sprayer full of what I could only guess was some sort of pesticide. There were swarms of hornets flying around the vendor who was pump, pumping away. While some hornets flew away others flew in so there was a fog of pesticide shrouding the area. The heavy mist settled on the mysterious loaves. *My God, who would eat that?* Never the less, the locals were coming up and buying the loaves without any regard to its toxic veneer. I am not talking fiddle-dee-dee hornets as in Alaska; I am talking long-legged-long-bodied, striped-tummy and angry -- Indian hornets! Once I saw what was happening, I moved away as quickly as I could.

We went into various shops and I ended up purchasing one brass pot for the latrine; one bar of Palmolive soap (sold everywhere and entrapping a forever sweet-scented memory) and a colorful piece of pink fabric for bathing. I also picked up a few things for Charlotte and when we had all bought what we needed, we began our walk back to the mission.

I was mystified by my déjà vu moment but then, this was India and India was a mystical land.

Sharing the rooms with Adam, Ron and William was the Australian named Paul. Paul was not on the drive but would be on the course with the rest of us. He was the carpenter that almost ran me over at the tool shed. Bhante wasted no time in putting him to work to build, repair or do anything carpentry-else on the grounds. Paul was a true Aussie; he had the "g'day mate" accent, bushy brown mustache and wore outback clothing, including the original bush hat. He was friendly and took on the chores of carpentry with great enthusiasm; that is, *at the beginning of the course*.

Within a few days of our arrival, Renata showed up. We were all gathered in the temple for informal meditations and there she was. Bhante had been waiting for her. He had talked with her many times before and was insistent that she needed to attend this course. She was Austrian and had come and gone at the mission many, many times throughout several years. She was also the oldest in our group being in her mid-thirties at the time. She was the most scholarly of all of us, being knowledgeable in religion, cultures, languages and she could talk your ear off on any subject, invited or otherwise.

Renata could also sit down to hot-hot curry dishes, chomping on an explosive green chili pepper while spooning in scorching main dishes as though it were porridge. After my experience back in England it was absolutely incredible to watch her eat. I stared in wonderment. *Was not heat - heat? How did she do it and make it look so good?*

During the next few days of our arrival a few other people came to attend the informal meditations and ceremonies that were being held in the temple with Bhante. The visitors were from the hostel and because the course was not officially open they were all welcome. A few of the visitors expressed an interest in attending the course. Gerome and his friend Jean Pere were accepted to attend the course although they didn't live in the group quarters; they lived in a cave, under a tree or something akin to that on the property. I never visited their sleeping quarters. Gerome was from New York and resembled, at least to me, what I would term a Greenwich Village beatnik. Jean Pere was Lebanese and had a bushy black beard and dark humble eyes. He was by far the quietest and most humble person on the course.

There were two others that had expressed an interest in attending the course, one was an Australian girl and the other was a British man. They had both been on a meditation retreat under the auspices of a famous meditation instructor. These were ten-day courses in silent Vipassana Meditation. The young lady was persistent in her effort to be accepted on the course and would not be discouraged. Bhante finally relented and accepted their attending but he was reluctant from the start. "I cannot tell them no." was what Bhante would say. The young Brit was allowed on the course but he was not allowed to do any meditation. The Australian girl roomed with Renata in the front room of the ladies dormitory. The Brit went to stay with the guys next door.

Along with the gathering of course mates and preparation in general, the announcement that no couples would be allowed to cohabitate unless they were married brought about wedding plans for Duff and Aime as well as Gunther and Charlotte. It was a busy time for us and I was feeling much better by now. So, when Ron called out that Duff had to go into Delhi to take care of wedding plans and anyone that wanted could come, I said "wait for me!"

I really had no sense in going to Delhi; I was still barely recovered from the drive and should have just stayed back at the mission. It was just too tempting, going into the city and trying authentic Indian cooking. Charlotte could come on this one so we got ready and met up near the vans.

After the fruit in Pakistan I was not going to take any chances in eating. India was no different than other places in that we had to get to know which places catered either to the soft-as-silk stomachs of the western tourists or the cast-iron-bellies of the locals. In time we could adapt and grow but for now, I couldn't take any chances and since Duff knew the safe cafes… Then there was just getting to see New Delhi for the first time; who could say no?

Somewhere along our trip or in her packing, Charlotte, ever efficient, had acquired a small booklet on India and had been reading about New Delhi so on the drive into the city she told me all about Connaught Place or CP, which was where we were heading. CP is one of the largest commercial and business centers in New Delhi and was built between 1929 and 1932. It is a huge round-about with many tiers, like that of a wheel with spokes going out from a central cog.

"It states here that we should not pay the beggars. They are professionals and make more than the average Indian citizen," Charlotte showed me a passage in her guide book.

"Hmm, that's Interesting." I said as I leaned in to read the passage.

When we got to the circle, the traffic was congested and uncontrolled; exiting and entering without warning. Bikes with their jingling bells, taxis with their horns quacking; lorries of all kinds and the festively colored buses, with people hanging from windows and perilously riding on the rear bumper -- all were honking and gesturing simultaneously. The occasional oxcart and elephant passed through the circle as well. It was a smooth pandemonium; predictable only by its erratic nature.

Chapter 29

When we parked, sure enough we were surrounded by tiny children in rags and filth, hands extended outward with palms up begging for "baksheesh". They looked so forlorn that I could not believe they had more money than a lot of Indians. I gave one child a small coin and that is all it took for me to be surrounded by a flock of beggars of both genders and of all ages that pushed and pecked at me. They didn't relent either. I moved left; they shuffled, shuffled left. I moved forward; they fox trotted forward with me. I don't know how I got out of the crowd but most likely I was freed when another bleeding heart came along and did the same.

Crossing the few blocks necessary to get to our destination was even more challenging. In crossing the block one had to look right, left, right, again and again; then just go for it by a quick run to the other side. There was never a time that some vehicle was not passing by. Up, down, dodge and dart; run like hell…

"Hey, there's Duff." I pointed to a cafe across the street where I saw him sipping coffee on the veranda. I guess that he had completed his errands a little sooner than he had expected and was waiting patiently for us. He flagged us over and we all gathered round to sit down. He guaranteed that good Indian cooking was prepared here and that I was safe in ordering. So, I ordered what Duff recommended for me which was hot, almost too hot for my palate. I mixed in a lot of rice and managed to get it all down. It was not as sweet and tasty as the southern Indian style of cooking that I had tasted in London. This was more hot than flavorful. Different areas of India produced different flavors for curry dishes and I found myself disappointed with the northern Indian seasonings; preferring southern flavors over the northern hot spicy dishes. It was just how I saw it back then. I loved chutney for enhancing curries flavor but there wasn't any served with the dishes. It was something I would need to get used to.

We all sat around eating together; talking about the wedding that was coming up and watching the general public pass by as we enjoyed the hot sun from the café deck. Sight-seeing would have to wait until the first official day off from the course, the wedding plans were going on and we had to get back to the mission after our lunch.

That night the rumbling began all over again and my bowels released their raging blow-torch blaze of elimination. I was on fire; burning from top to bottom, literally. *Not again!* Late that night, after the last latrine visit I came into my room and collapsed on the bed, too sick to even grab the mosquito netting to cover me. As I slept countless mosquitoes attacked my face, landing and taking off throughout the night. I could feel them stinging but did nothing about it.

The next day, my forehead was covered with bumps and my eyes were almost swollen shut. I went to breakfast and sat there on the bench feeling half alive; I had developed a sore throat as well as not being able to sit too comfortably owing to all the enraged colon activity. It took days to get over this bout.

CHAPTER 30

After Delhi, I stayed close to home and got better. The mission seemed to have that effect on my health. My recovery from all the bouts of illness was relatively quick and in spite of all the adjustments and illnesses, we all began to prepare for the weddings of Duff and Aime and Charlotte and Gunther. This would mark the commencement of the course, which was scheduled for October 31st. I got together with Aime to talk about a wedding outfit for Aime. She didn't have a dress but had some blue satin fabric she wanted to have made into a top and she had white fabric for a skirt. A couple of us had volunteered to help in creating pattern pieces based on Aime's description and then cut out the fabric to the pattern we had fashioned.

We took the cut pieces to the tailor's shop and *of course, of course, no problem* they assured us that they could have them sewn and ready by tomorrow at noon. We showed up at eleven the next day and there lay the pieces in the same heap that we had left them the day before. Aime was furious and demanded they begin sewing immediately. The gentleman picked up the fabric and began sewing. What began was a "sew as you go" event. Pieces were cut here and there, the skirt was tweaked a bit and in no time a top and skirt evolved. Amazing! What appeared a disaster at 11:00, turned out to be a wedding combo by noon.

"I cannot image how zay were going to sew zat together!" cried Aime as she watched over the tailor with her furrowed brow and pointing fingers.

Her thick French accent added a little humor to an otherwise stressful situation. "What eez zat? No, cut zat off!"

*Hmm; a*s I watched Aime direct the sewing, I got to thinking that maybe we might have made a *few* technical errors in the pattern design. I didn't say a word; I was just grateful for the sewing skills of that gentleman; with his huge scissors and trestle sewing machine he snipped, peddled and puffed his way to a small miracle.

Fortunately, we had already done the shopping in Kabul for Charlotte's dress and ring so there was little to no preparation involved for her wedding ensemble. Garlands of marigolds were made for both the brides and grooms and both Charlotte and Aime wore a crown of marigolds. The men were dressed in white pants and shirt -- Indian style.

It was a solemn yet joyful Buddhist wedding held in the temple beneath the altar of Lord Buddha. The two couples knelt on the floor with their palms together in prayer position. Bhante and the other monks sat facing them and we all sat behind the wedding party. There was chanting, bowing, incense and water. The ceremony took an hour or so. When it was finished we all rose and exited the temple.

As we came out, well-wishers tossed fresh flowers over the newlyweds. The soft petals settled on the veranda floor carpeting the area with specks of light pinks, creams and bright marigold. It was a warm sunny day and we had a joyful celebration, with good food and lots of conversation. During the drive, I had come to know Charlotte well and knew how much in love she was with Gunther. Aime was just as in love with Duff (go figure!). I really hoped the best for them all. I couldn't help but think *what a wonderful way to start the course.*

CHAPTER 31

In retrospect, I think the course had really begun the moment we boarded the ferry in Dover; there it was final in our collection of people, gear and vans. We were all together on a journey and whether we knew each other or not, we would have to learn to work together. Likes and dislikes would rise to the surface almost instantly as we worked our way through the necessary activities of daily living.

Of course most of us had met in England but for the most part our England experience was not of a group but strangers meeting; going here and there, always rushed with little time to visit or work as a unit. We all had distinct personalities. Duff's main activities throughout the drive would be to avoid Bhante, guide us to India, eat; not cook, drink and leave the clean-up to the rest of us. In retrospect, he fulfilled a vital role. We enjoyed each other, worked together and laughed a lot together. We could settle each other down when necessary and keep each other awake in the long drive. Some of us cooked; some of us cleaned, but we all helped each other when we needed to.

The mission picked up where the driving left off; the degree of spiritual intensity in India was due in part to the long drive and its gradual breaking down of barriers that we would normally hold dear to ourselves in the outside world with its daily distractions.

We couldn't shut the door and say, I will never speak to that person again. No, we had to grin and bear it, sometimes grousing a little, but continuing to depend on each other even if, at times, from afar. Our banding together through mountain passes and Khyber bandits was our beginning.

And it was that night of the wedding which marked the first official meditation of the **Opportunity for Serious Seekers** course of a lifetime. Bhante and Gambhiro sat in front of us. There was a young Frenchman named Louis that had come to India seeking to be a monk but Bhante would not accept him as a novice. He also sat in the front area. Although he was on the grounds during the course he was not a classmate. He did meditate with us; I guess you could say he was semi-attached.

Walking into the temple the first night, I was lucky enough to snag a cushion and a column to prop against. We began the course with a ceremony for blessings and prayers of success. During the ceremony Bhante and the monks chanted prayers. Bhante had a bowl of water in front of him and was stirring it with a twig. As they reached certain points in the prayers, he would flick the branch out and have the blessed water lightly sprinkle over us. We kept our hands in prayer position during the ceremony.

At one point Bhante spoke of the five precepts, which we would all commit to. Charlotte had typed up all the necessary documents, from which we all read or repeated. Adhering to the five precepts was a recommendation to us. Bhante always explained, "You must know for yourself. The proof is in the pudding." He also explained a little about the chants/prayers we were performing: The Buddha -- Yay cha Buddha...The Dharma -- Yay cha Dharma...The Sangha -- Yay cha Sangha, and so on. He was clear and reverent in his dialogue.

On the first night, we made the solemn commitment to abstain from; harming living beings, taking things not freely given, sexual misconduct, false speech, intoxicating drinks and drugs. These five precepts were commitments we were making to ourselves for self-growth and it was not prescribed with a heavy hand. This was a solemn event for us and I was personally excited to begin, yet fearful of the unknown.

"For success in your efforts, it is important to remember the three P's; persistence, perseverance and patience." He held up three fingers as he quietly related these words of encouragement. From this point we began the formal instruction in the meditative process.

He had just instructed us in the sending of loving kindness and compassion; goodwill and good wishes to all beings when he spoke. "Do not think the meditation begins with the observation of breath. The meditation begins with the sending of loving kindness and compassion; good will and good wishes to all beings. Take some time on this and concentrate. When you have been able to do this, then you may begin with the observation of breath."

He then paused as we began. Several minutes later he began his instruction on the observation of breath and we began the second part of the meditation. We meditated for an hour or more.

My first meditation was the typical struggle with all kinds of thoughts, emotions, aches and itches. My lower limbs have never been flexible and without the cushion to sit on my knees would have stuck straight up rather than relax downward. My body was stiff and uncomfortable in the new position and I fidgeted as quietly as possible. The green lights shone down on us and the clock on the wall next to the shrine area was tick tock, ticking away. *How strange to have a clock that was so loud in the temple.* It was a cheap round, plastic, gold-rimmed standard clock, nothing special but it became a focal point of agitation. I didn't dare open my eyes to see the time; but how I wanted to.

When we were to end we began our chants and prayers ending with "May all beings be well and happy." The first meditation of the course had finished. We rose and bowed and said good night to Bhante.

I slipped on my flip flops which were just outside the temple doors and walked to my room. It was dark now and there were a few lights next to the buildings that softly lit the way. They were of low wattage so beyond the path all was dark. Several from the group were gathered along the path and I said good-night as I passed by them.

I went into my room, pulled out an aerogramme or two and plopped myself on my bed. I wanted to write about the first night mostly to review it in my mind. As it was, there wasn't anything to say. It was a struggle at best and I was tired. Outside I could hear the others saying their good nights or talking together about going to the hostel for chai and conversation. Their footsteps faded into the night air and all was quiet. Could I do this? Was I up to the task? Only time would tell. I wrote my letters and got into my sleeping bag, said a prayer and fell to sleep.

I slept well that night. In the morning, about twenty minutes before Gambhiro began ringing the bell to wake us, the rooster began flapping his wings and crowing. The first night I spent on the mission and heard the rooster's terrible thumping and flapping, I threw open my sleeping bag; ready to run. When he started crowing, I realized what was happening and lay back down shaking and trembling but grateful that I hadn't run into a wall or stubbed my toe.

I wrapped myself in my friendly sleeping bag and waited. It was pitch-dark and I wasn't ready to get up. Once Gambhiro passed by the dorms ringing the bell, I rose and went to the toilettes. It was always a dark walk this early but it is where we usually said our good mornings to one another. Once finished with the latrine, we would gather around the water faucet to wash up and brush our teeth. From here, I ran back to the room, picked up my shawl and headed to the temple. This was the routine for the duration of the course.

We were all arriving within a few seconds of each other kicking off our sandals and entering into the temple en masse. Quietly we found our spots and sat down. My favorite column and cushion were available and once again I sat down and prepared to meditate.

As we all sat, Bhante entered smiling and saying good morning to us. We all replied, "Good morning, Bhante" and he took his place in front of us; our morning meditation began. The clock was still ticking. Only once did I ever notice the clock was silent. I honestly thought that I had perhaps finally conquered my obsession with its ticking, but it turned out to need new batteries. Once the dead batteries were replaced it continued without interruption. I really hated that clock.

About fifteen minutes before we completed our morning meditation, as the daylight was creeping into the temple, I heard a strange far-off cry. I had never heard such a sound and could not for the life of me figure out what it was. It wasn't the sound of anything in danger, rather more like the calling out of a name – as a mother calling to a lost child. I listened as the sound grew closer and gathered to a chorus of lamentations.

Just a few days later right after morning meditation, when we were leaving the temple Siraj came running up shouting "The peacocks, the peacocks!" Duff bent down and picked up a rock and ran with Siraj to the back gardens. Those haunting cries were peacocks. Most of the times they were outside our four walls but on this morning they had made their way into our territory and were now set to eat all of Siraj's hard work. It was hard for me to imagine those beautiful creatures being unwelcome anywhere but sadly they were pests that feasted on plants and in particular well-tended and delicious gardens. What a surprise for me to watch the commotion, and seeing those beautiful birds, their weighty plumes bouncing heavily behind them, as they fled the mission. Jumping, then flapping wildly they lifted up to the high back wall and left the area. Every morning beyond our stone wall, the cry of the peacocks threatened assuring me another morning meditation was almost over. We finished with, "May all beings be well and happy", rose and quietly walked to the doorway; breakfast was just around the corner.

Chapter 32

The sweet smell of the fire and toasted chapattis floated up to greet us in the cool morning mist. Chris became head cook for the breakfast meal since he was not meditating with us. Oh, what wonderful smells they were; along with brewing tea and steaming oat porridge there was the sweet smell of damp earth. We still had some jam, biscuits and other western delicacies from our drive in the earlier days of the course so we ate quite well for a while.

The sun, as it rose, illuminated the back wall; creating angled shadows. Wow, what a beautiful sight! It heightened my perceptions and every pore in my body consumed the moment. I wrapped my shawl tightly around me and ate as much as I could. We weren't too talkative with one another early in the morning; we mainly ate and quietly talked about what the day's activities were.

There is a certain smoky smell that can transport me back to mornings in India; as though I am still there in the back kitchen, shivering, as I tug at my shawl; waiting in line for hot tea, a toasty chapatti and a bowl of steaming porridge. Meal in hand, I find a place to sit and share this sacred meal with my classmates. Incense does the same to me. Give me Sandalwood, nag champa or frankincense and I am back at the mission, hearing the wall clock tick-tock ticking away.

After eating, we washed the dishes in the outdoor sink. We used ashes or sometimes a store purchased powdered cleaning compound. Everyone cleaned their own plates and then someone would finish the pots and pans. At first it was a jumble of clamoring and sprays of water but as time went on we became synchronized and the routine flowed.

In one of our earlier meetings in the temple, the daily schedule of the course and the chores that needed to be done were discussed. Charlotte and I received the task of kitchen stewards. We would oversee the daily kitchen tasks and make a cooking schedule.

Those of us not cooking lunch had garden chores; the men kept busy with carpentry while Duff did a lot of driving for Bhante; we all had some task. The physical work was based on our need to "Balance the energy"; as Bhante put it. During the morning work activities Bhante would often walk the grounds with Gambhiro. He would smile at all of us and ask us how we were. He would ask about the lunchtime meal and direct the men for a carpentry project or would instruct Gambhiro to inform us of some new activity.

Aussie Paul was put to work constructing free-standing walls for the Seema room. They were waste high and about three and a half feet wide. Once constructed, they were painted green and taken into the Seema room. Each of us was assigned permanent seating areas in the room. The first day of our afternoon meditation in the room, Bhante took each one of us to our place. He then showed us how to pull the walls around us creating a small personalized meditation hut. In this little space we would spend many an hour in silent contemplation. I received a corner cube.

So there we all were; working together on various chores of cooking, weeding or building. On fasting days we might take on a larger project such as making jam or cleaning the kitchen cupboards. These things took a little more time and a fasting day was good for that.

After the cleanup from breakfast, lunch prep began. There would be two of us assigned for the task. It was a regular routine without any fanfare. Charlotte and I, as the kitchen stewards, devised a schedule for cooking and menus as well. The menu wasn't difficult. It was just like back in Botley at the Myat Shi's. What Saraj, the farmer brought us was what was cooked. It was usually the standard cauliflower. We had lentils and rice and always chapattis. The additional rice and soy sauce from our trip made our meal filling and flavorful. As time went by, we were able to get more lentils and rice from the nearest rations shop.

When there were a few items that needed to be purchased in the market, Charlotte, Aime or I (always two of us) would walk the mile into town to make the necessary purchases. The carrots were growing, aubergine just barely showing, but boy was there cauliflower. There was a field in front of the Seema Room that had mustard growing. It would be harvested and the seeds taken to the vendor who would produce mustard oil, which we would use for cooking. It was Siraj's duty to take the mustard seeds to the oil producer because he knew the reputable ones. Before the field went to seed some of the greens would be harvested and cooked.

When we did have to go to town for a few items we always found time for Nescafe with milk and sugar; we'd visit a little while drinking and then head back with the staples.

Just beyond the last block of vendors, heading home, there were ruins of old buildings that we passed through; sometimes we would stop here to eat or visit. Pigs roamed freely eating whatever they could find. With no sewer system in the town you might be able to imagine what the pigs feasted on. When I first had this explained to me I was sickened, but as time went by and we wore down the path between the small village and the temple, the pigs were just another part of the landscape. *Never eat pork in India* was duly noted in my things *not* to do in India file.

One time, after Aime and I had finished shopping and were heading home, we decided to sit down in the ruins and talk for awhile. We were talking about our lives and how we managed to get to India. It was a beautiful sunny morning and we didn't plan to stay long but Aime was sharing with me the most remarkable story about her journey to India.

Aime had literally walked to India; taking rides only when offered. She had an amazing story to tell, which I hope she shares with the world someday.

When we were through talking we got up to leave; walking merrily along the path laughing and having a pleasant little time. All of a sudden, as we turned a corner, we almost bumped right into a man who was performing a vulgar act on himself. He had been hiding and watching us the whole time that we had been sitting and visiting and obviously he was turned on. When we came face to face with him we jumped back in shock. I was startled and began to laugh at how ridiculous the man looked, but Aime picked up a stone to defend us and said in her broken English, "Aaah, you dae*rr*ty mahn". She hurled the rock at him -- he leaned away from us and ducked without letting go of himself -- if you know what I mean. We ran down the path to the temple. All the while, he kept shouting to us, "Meme Sahib, meme sahib" then saying something to us in Hindi.

For whatever reason, I found the whole thing humorous. Aime was flustered and angry and kept saying, "Zat dae*rr*ty mahn. Zat dae*rr*ty mahn." When we were well beyond him, Aime told me that he was offering us money to finish the job for him.

"Hey, wait a minute. How much did he say he'd pay?" I joked as we ran away.

We hurried down the path and crossed into the mission via the archway. No sooner were we on the promenade, heading towards the kitchen when Charlotte pointed upwards. There on the thin branch of the kumquat tree sat a beautiful multi-colored exotic bird; silent and regal, feasting on the small, fresh kumquats. "It's the Fruit Loops bird!" I shouted out. Charlotte put her finger to her mouth to shush me so it would not fly off. I am not sure what the name of the bird was but it was so striking in its soft pastels and long beak. What a contrast to what lay just outside the mission walls!

We told our story at the lunch meal; it was humorous, vulgar and alarming all at the same time and life went on at the mission. I never saw him again on any walk; I figured he probably had learned to hide a little better.

Chapter 33

After an evening meditation just a few evenings into the course while I was heading back to my room, I saw Duff speaking with a young woman. She was of medium to smallish build and was wearing an orange turban-type head dress and clothing. As I walked by, I was introduced to Katy. She had just arrived back from the mountains and would be my roommate. I said hello to her and she stared back at me. *What was that look?* I continued to walk to my/our room while Katy stood on the promenade; then she turned around and walked toward the temple. I wasn't quite sure of it but I could swear she almost growled at me.

Katy came to the room later that evening. She had been in the temple speaking with Bhante. She had had an upsetting experience with a guru and wanted Bhante to say a few prayers for her. As we got to know each other better, she told me what had happened to her. She left the mission for the mountains once Bhante had left for Europe the previous summer. While traveling she met a "holy" man that turned out to not be so "holy" and she came back to the mission as quickly as possible once she discovered his evil nature. She was rattled by her circumstances and from time to time, while we would be talking, she would begin chanting to the Buddha. Within a week or two she was back to her kind of normal.

Katy was from Spain and had met Bhante a year or two earlier and had come to the mission at that time. She ended up staying and became a devotee of Bhante's. She was a delightful person; full of energy and always running about doing things but in an anxious manner so that she always seemed to trip up or would have something come out the wrong way when she spoke. She told great stories; with waving of hands and eyes popping out.

Katy was a great roommate, a lot different from me in that she did not put things in order according to my standards. Nag, nag, nag; I was good at that. At one point she shouted out, "Shut up Liza, you're not my mother!"

We both laughed and I quit being such a nag-maybe. She became a confidante and wonderful friend.

Our bedroom window came to be the short cut for anyone wishing to shorten their front to back or back to front walk. We would keep the window open most of the time in the day and there would be a knock or quick "Hello" as someone came in or out of our room. Katy and I would always use the shortcut.

We would smoke our bidis (a pinch of tobacco rolled into a leaf from the Beetle Nut tree) from the window and visit or joke with anyone that was walking along the back path. Paagal was always a visitor. He and I became close during the course and he often popped his head in and carried on lengthy nonsensical conversations with me. Katy sometimes shooed him away but he would always sneak back and peak around the window to see if she had left the room. If she was gone, he'd make a face and wave at her bed, then pick up where he had left off earlier; he was always good for a laugh or two.

As night would roll in we'd close the window and tuck in for the night. No one came through in the evening. We'd hear the quiet talking in front then the sound of footsteps headed for the hostel. Time for sleep.

Chapter 34

"Oh my God, what is that!?" I asked Gambhiro.

A bunch of us were sitting around the small porch off the guest room when Siraj came up and handed Gambhiro one of those mysterious brown loaves I had seen being sprayed with DDT!

"Brown sugar" he replied.

I was horrified.

Gambhiro went on to explain that Siraj bought the brown sugar from a good vendor so it was safe to use. I hated the taste, which was pungent. I can't describe it; it was molasses, but not; it was sweet, but not, it had DDT on it, but maybe not?

Just a few evenings before this, I had been jolted out of my sleep by severe pain in my abdomen. I rolled out of bed clutching my stomach and hurried to the temple. Each step caused a sharp pain to shoot through my body. I was bent over and staggering when I spotted Bhante at the temple door. He was just closing up for the night. He looked up and saw me and smiled as I approached him. As I came closer he realized something was wrong. I could only gasp, "Bhante, my stomach-pain."

He quickly put me under the blue light in the therapy area. I lay on a mattress and the blue light was placed about three feet from the center of my pain. Slowly the pain went away and I left for bed again. A few nights later the pain returned but instead of going to Bhante, I lay in my bed and concentrated all the energy I could into repeating, "Blue Light, Blue Light". Soon the pain vanished. When I talked about the pains with the group the Australian girl said it sounded like the Chakra in my solar plexus was being opened up. Bhante had said he thought it was an ulcer attack.

Now, with the delivery of the toxic loaf, I reflected back on when the stomach pains came; it seemed that it might be related to eating something that might have contained this sweetener. It seemed more credible than a lofty Chakra opening up or an ulcer attack. I made sure to avoid all sweetened dishes of questionable ingredients.

The discomfort never came back and I never found out what it was but I felt certain that the quick recovery was due, in part, to Bhante's strong presence; just like never being disturbed by spiders, rats, cockroaches or things that could frighten the heck out of me and were everywhere in India. Never once did any of the mentioned creatures run across my bedroom floor; we had a few ants but they were small and kept to a neat little path on the wall and went out a tiny little hole. Even the mosquitoes never bothered me after that one evening I didn't cover myself with the netting, and which I never used. I remember thinking about this-where did all the mosquitoes go? And it is only now that I think about the missing creepy crawlies.

CHAPTER 35

There were so many days that ran right into each other as routines became smooth. Often I craved privacy or silence; just to sit for a moment free of any thoughts, responsibilities or inner struggles. There was a place out back by the fire pit that I could sit from time to time and just stare without thought. It was where we rinsed our dishes, which created a small canal that irrigated the small leafed spinach and lemon grass patches that bordered our cooking area.

I would take the small bench and sit to watch the chipmunks as they scurried over to the large metal bowl of leftovers left for Cookie and Blackie. The chipmunks would fight over the huge bowl; the alpha chipmunk ate first while the others jockeyed for position by chasing each other away. It was a tiny little circus act. Soon Cookie and Blackie showed up and the chipmunks hurried away. The observation was mindless yet I couldn't help but think how big the bowl was and how there was no need to fight over the leftovers. Eventually they all ate and all that fighting was just a waste of time. I didn't think we humans in general displayed much more awareness than the poor chipmunks. If the chipmunks wised up just a little, they might possibly overtake us in evolution.

I got up and went to my room to gather up my laundry and headed toward the well. During the siesta period, we washed our clothes or bathed or took care of other personal business. Our bathing and laundry was done up at the well, which I was told, never went dry; not even in times of the most severe draught. The pump would be turned on and water would fill a huge cement trough. The one end of the trough was open in the middle so that the water would tumble down into a small cement pool. Here we would wash our clothes or bathe.

The magenta colored cloth that I had purchased was stitched together at the ends making a circle of fabric. I would step into the sewn cloth, pull it up; tighten and tuck it around my chest. All tucked in, I would make my way to the well. We women had all purchased our own fabric and as I approached the well it resembled a tiny field of colorful wildflowers gathered round the water fall.

One at a time, as the water tumbled into the small wading pool we would stand under the rush of water and hold open the fabric to allow our bodies to be showered; a portable shower stall of sorts. It was all quite private and the water was always warm. There was never a time that washing was ever a problem. There were clothes lines for drying near the dorms and on the roof. Drying didn't take long and hygiene was never a concern.

After siesta time was over our afternoon meditation was held in the Seema Room. Afternoon meditation was always tough for me. The beautiful white one-storied structure was just beyond the dorms, on the other side of the path that lead to the backyard. I passed it at least twice every day because it was also on the way to the toilets.

An indescribable cloud of weighty silence surrounded the Seema Room. It was a single storied cement structure; painted a brilliant white There were small white pillars about three feet high bordering the front of the building. It had a quality not unlike the mosque in Herat and yet it differed. Just walking by it always stirred something inside me. I always took the time to study it whenever I passed. A thin flowering tree grew beside the doorway and there were two tall skinny windows that flanked the narrow door. The windows and doors were painted dark green -- a clear glass light bulb, barely visible, dangled from the tree branches that spread out and above the entry. I always felt the urge to jump up and shout "Hello!" when I passed by. It was as though something was going on in there but whatever it was, I couldn't see it. Here we spent, every day, for at least a continuous hour and a half, in sitting meditation and then to walking meditation for another hour.

I was always a little weary in entering the Seema Room. First it had that heavy silence and secondly there would be all the stalls, empty and waiting for us. We would joke with each other, "See you in Nirvana" type jokes as we entered and walked to our private green squares. I stepped into the small cube and closed the walls of green plywood around me and sat down. *Cosmic Consciousness or bust...* We all became quiet and Bhante would enter later.

Bhante sat in the center of the room while we sat around the walls. As I sat in the cube meditating I enjoyed the quiet. Although I enjoyed the quiet, I was myself not quieted. I had discovered a small opening at the top of the room. It was a small rectangular shaped vent with a screen over it. It was off to my right and up where the roof line and wall met. I had to twist a little and look up to see it. Outside that small vent I could see branches from the massive tree that grew next to the building; I would watch the branches stir and see the leaves wave back and forth. They made a nice rustling sound.

Whatever distractions that came and went nothing stopped the length of this meditation. In the beginning there could be "good" days for meditating where time would fly by but usually just knowing that we had X amount of time in one sitting was torture for me. *How do I measure ninety minutes? How does ninety minutes feel? How long was I on the first part of the meditation -- if it was, say ten minutes, then I have eighty left and how can I break that down into increments that will help me?* Then after realizing I was pondering all of this I gently would bring myself back to observing the breath. Green in -- impurities out...And so on...Sometimes Bhante would snore during the meditation or sometimes he quietly would walk around peering into our cubes to gauge our progress. At times he would speak about effort encouraging us to return to the meditation but never force it or control it; just return.

In truth, I feared Nirvana or Cosmic Consciousness -- *as if!* I had a boyfriend back home and I fretted at times about it; if I achieved this status, I would have to give up my former life and I really didn't want to give it all up just yet. Such considerations chit chatted in my mind as I pushed my body forward to lean close to the green wall, eyes closed interspersed with "Green light, green light, green light" pleadings. So many conversations drifted in and out.

"If your mind wonders, just return to the observation of breath. Observe the air as it passes into the nose brushing your upper lip. Do not force yourself, just return." Bhante's voice would softly beckon me back.

After the meditation, there was a small break and then on to the walking meditation back in the Seema Room. We gathered in a line around the walls and Bhante demonstrated what we were to do. We were to concentrate on the feet and observe in mantra fashion the *lifting* and *putting* of our feet as we walked around the room. The room had a slight archway between the two small areas and while we were walking, one time, I peeked up at everyone. I don't know if I was the only one that couldn't resist a peak at the procession but I just couldn't help myself. *How did we all look?* Ron was walking with an exaggerated lift almost like giant marching steps. Because we were all clustered together the steps weren't long but high. He was looking down with an expression that was between terror and concentration. The Frenchman walked with his hands behind his back, his legs were stiff and his lower lip was pouting out, his eyes furrowed as he stared down. It appeared as though he were reprimanding his feet. Duff was stiff and I wondered what dance step it was that he looked like he was performing, the cha in the cha, cha, cha, or a trot from the fox trot? I think it was Adam that hit his head when he walked right into the arch; it made a loud thump in our otherwise quiet walkabout. Everyone had their own style in their effort. Of course, we women looked intent and graceful. I never looked after that, it just didn't seem fair. The room grew hotter and hotter as we walked and walked; *lifting* and *putting* our feet around the tiny rooms of the building.

Finally when we were done we would half stumble half walk out of the Seema Room into the fresh air. One day after this lengthy effort, wouldn't you know, who should be there to greet us but Paagal. There he was, lying on the ground in front of us just at the edge of the mustard field, no more than ten feet from us. He was in a reclining Buddha pose with a blade of tall grass between his teeth. He had a -- *you poor fools* look on his face. Then he waved to us as and rolled over to prone position and raised one leg over the other, swinging that bony little leg back and forth as though he had not a care in the world; he rested his hands behind his head and gazed to the heavens humming a tune. As we passed by him, he grabbed at our ankles and in his gibberish he would call out to us as though he was pleading for our help. Then he would roll over, get up and dust himself off, chuckling and shrugging all the while. Once in a while, he would bring his hands together and bow to us or sometimes he would follow me calling out "meme sahib, meme sahib" rattling off a desperate dialogue of God only knows what.

Paagal never made much sense and no one ever knew exactly what he was talking about at any time. In retrospect, I am certain he was a genuine "Fool for Christ" or the Hindu equivalent to that. The "fools" as they are called are found in all spiritual pathways. Paagal denotes the word crazy which indeed points to the term of "Holy Crazy One". Seriously, he was too good at his foolishness to not have a purpose. He loved to make fun of us and acted out so many western stereotypes that it was a wonder he had never been out of India. The actions of the "Fools" are to mock us and this society we have fashioned after ourselves. A true fool has already done the necessary work on his or her own self and have a way of zinging that reflects back to humanity its stupidity. Anyone within their intentional perimeter is affected/effected by their outlandish actions. This a sacred being; stronger than innocence and clear in virtue.

After awhile, we took the walking meditation outside under the Bodhi tree. On rainy days we would return to the Seema Room. I have to say here and now that as the course went on I mostly skipped out of this meditation and performed my "walking-whatever" to a local café by the bus stop for a cup of hot Nescafe with a serving of poories and chickpeas at the bus stop. I would get back just in time to wiggle back in line right before the meditation ended. If I could talk someone into going with me, so much the merrier; we would both eat our fill of bus stop food, talk and hurry home. Bhante was never present at the walking meditation so it was pretty easy. We all had our escapes or struggles, no one judged. It was life on the course.

After we had just finished one of our walking meditations Paagal shuffled over to the Bodhi Tree. He proceeded to mock us; bowing and strutting his way around and around; walking slowly feigning reverence and rapture. I can still see the sunset behind him; silhouetting his shape; that big turbaned head and skinny match-figure body of his as he nodded and moved around. Tea time came and went; he stayed there under the Bodhi Tree.

When he decided he was done he came down the path snickering at us, then he would run over to one of us and do his yanking of shirt sleeve, eyeballs popping out and anxious; rattling off some mumbo jumbo. Then, off he'd go shaking it off and on to Act II somewhere else on the mission.

"If you are not able to perform the walking meditation all the time, then try to concentrate on left foot/right foot as you walk. Observe your feet in this way as you go about your daily chores." Bhante recommended.

I applied his suggestion immediately and as the left/right stepping took hold, I had a few days of seeing everything that moved through the left/right walking pattern. The ducks were walking in the pathway and I could only watch their feet and internally observe *left/right, left/right, left/right* as they waddled about; everyone I watched, all I saw was the movement of their feet and their left/right walking. As I grew more centered in *my* walking meditation, I was able to let the rest go. I have been doing the walking meditation almost without a break, for over 37 years. So, you see I may have skipped out on the Bodhi Tree but never really escaped the discipline.

After walking meditation we had a small break, then tea time. While we drank our tea we had our readings, which were from natural healing books; covering topics on health, cleansings, auras, and, of course, Color therapy. When Bhante came and sat with us he would ask us, as a particular book was being read, "How do they know this is correct or what makes them know this?" His point was that, once again, we should not take anyone's word on any subject; that we were to have first-hand experience before anything should be accepted as a Truth. Knowledge was good, we read and learned but his point was the necessity to have First-Hand Knowledge outside of linear concepts -- impressed yet not lost in the brain.

As a result of the readings, we were inspired to put ourselves on a cleansing and eliminating diet to see how it worked. It wasn't much different from what we ate except we got rid of salt and spicy seasonings, dairy, sweets, caffeine; other things that weighted down the digestion and retarded the elimination process. Aussie Paul once came to tea blindfolded; he had seen an aura. The covering of the eyes was to heighten his sensory perceptions with the hope of seeing more auras. It was comical but serious as well. We also moved our beds to face east; this was said to be the best way to sleep for optimum rest and good health. I changed back to the original head placement within a few days; it just didn't feel right. We tried just about everything as we read about various healing teachings.

On rainy days, we would go into the temple for the reading. Once, while one of us was reading about disease, the word organism came up. The reader, reading ever so efficiently said *orgasm*. To make matters worse as they tried to correct their misread they kept repeating variations of the word orgasm. Like *orgaa aasm*, or *orgas aa aaminism*. So once they got the word organism out, we had lost track of any serious healing information. Gambhiro, turned sideways and whispered, "Freudian Slip" and we all snickered.

CHAPTER 36

Like everything else I had become familiar with everyone's footsteps as they walked the back path. When I heard the hard flapping of flip flops pounding the back pathway, I leaned out and yelled "Here comes Pig Pen!"

It was Gunther. His flip flops had thick soles and they slapped up against his heels as he walked. I could hear him a mile away; his walk was so distinct from the rest. As he walked, he kicked up the dust, which reminded me of Pig Pen from the _Charlie Brown_ cartoons. Hence: Pig Pen. Gunther always smiled when I called him Pig Pen; he loved Charlie Brown -- the Snoopy character in particular. After being announced, he would come to the window and rest his head on the sill and pretend he was Snoopy spying into our room.

Gunther seemed such a strong soul. He had the ability to "work on himself" and it showed. "It doesn't matter" was his favorite response to things when I would talk to him about something upsetting. The thing is that someone else could say this and you would think, _Get real._ But not with Gunther, he said it with conviction and his own efforts provided the proof of it. He had a good sense of humor and enjoyed joking around but he also was a strong worker and remained much focused in any task.

"How's the oven coming along?" I asked him.

"It's almost finished and we should be baking in it soon."

The guys were making an oven at the outdoor cooking area. It would allow us to bake breads and other items. They had worked hard on the project and were just about done.

We were all excited because Adam's Aunt, Pat was visiting at the time and had offered to Bhante to make us Quiche Lorraine as the premier baking event for the virgin ovens. "I must make Quiche Lorraine for all of you!" She would tell us.

Money... No problem; she waved her hand as though tut-tutting the unworthy discussion of money; she would purchase all the ingredients.

"What is Quiche Lorraine?" I asked.

Adam's aunt went on to describe a mixture of cheese; eggs, cream, tomatoes and ham poured into a pie crust and baked. CHEESE, EGGS, CREAM, TOMATOES, HAM, PIE CRUST! *What!* Not only that, she would make TWO of them for us.

It had been nothing, or so it seemed, but lentils, rice and that ever present cauliflower for what seemed like ages. By the way, I don't know how many of you know this but along with the cockroach, it has been proven that cauliflower can survive a nuclear holocaust. What came first the cauliflower or the cockroach? I can go on and on about cauliflower and the years it took for me to stomach the taste of it after India. Bhante always boasted about how the mission lived on what it produced. It was appealing when I first heard him boast, how organic and all that, but once inside the gates, meditating for hours on end and you don't even have to ask what's for lunch because you can smell the cauliflower wafting through the mission air; well -- ugh! That's all I can say. We went through our driving staples quickly; no more soy sauce, white sugar, jam, western black tea or oatmeal.

When we ran out of tea, Bhante sent, via Gambhiro, a box of a good brand of black tea that he had in his small bedroom.

Unfortunately it had a dreadful taste. Rancid black tea is the worst but we had to drink it, after all we ate only what was on the mission -- rotten or otherwise.

Bhante's room was a floor to ceiling collection of papers, books and gifts such as the rancid tea. He could produce almost anything out of the room and although I could not figure out how he did it, he could place his hand instantly on anything archived in the chamber.

Now a meal of Quiche Lorraine; I was over the moon with anticipation.

I watched the ovens being built; anticipating the baking of Quiche Lorraine. Gunther worked away on the ovens, completing the task by spreading a thin sheet of cement to the walls. His face displayed serious concentration as he applied the finishing touches. Now it had to set up and then, by tomorrow they would be ready. *Yeah, baby!* I did a mindful hand rubbing, warming myself up by the great fire of gastronomical imagination. This was going to be good.

The rite of quiche preparation began with a trip to the market. Aunt Pat had prepared the list and I noticed the quiches called for at least a dozen eggs each-*what?!* That meant that we didn't have to portion, let's say, five eggs out to feed our large group; we would actually have one egg per person in the meal. Sometime earlier we had an abundance of eggs for a lunch meal so the head cook made deviled eggs. Unfortunately, he added an herb that was so bitter the eggs couldn't be eaten. Things like this just kept happening; so near and yet so far.

Off they went to the market and returned with a flourish of bags and wonderful Aunt Pat, always talking, walking ceremoniously to the back kitchen to prepare the meal. We all went about our various tasks, leaving her and Adam to the cooking.

The lunch bell rang and we all anxiously walked to the back kitchen area. When I got there I saw that something was wrong. It seemed the cement in the oven had not completely set up and as the oven got hotter and as the quiches baked away, the cement roof had chipped off and had fallen in little chunks into the quiches. They were ruined. Gunther looked crestfallen, Aunt Pat was apologizing and I was heartbroken. No quiche, it just can't be true, I thought. First, bitter deviled eggs and now this.

After a backup meal of that ever lovin' cauliflower and whatever, a few of us remained behind and picked through the quiche. The tiniest morsel of quiche, almost microscopic, had a crunch to it. I didn't care I was determined to eat at least one cement-free piece.

The quiche that had been on the bottom rack didn't fare any better. It didn't have large chunks of cement in it but had small grainy pieces peppered throughout. We tried that one as well but it was worse than the first one. It was easier to pick through the big chunks and try to brush away the pieces. Nothing worked -- it all crunched, but we sure tried. What desperation; rummaging through the ruins for one small morsel of anything remotely different from the standard mission fare. The karma gods were laughing.

Later that day, Gunther was back at work repairing and improving the oven. We never did have another quiche though; that was a one-trick pony. Aunt Pat left and I made a mental note to look up quiche of any kind when I got to the west. My list was growing.

CHAPTER 37

Bhante's weekly schedule was generous in that once a week we had a day off. There was always a morning meditation performed and breakfast served before we took off for Delhi. The gray Mercedes van was always used for the ten-mile drive and Duff usually drove. We would pop *Abbey Road* into the eight-track player and turn it up full blast, singing along to almost every song. My favorite was "*Here Comes the Sun*". God Bless George Harrison.

There we were driving, with the morning sunlight shining through the windows, to Delhi where food and all kinds of temptations awaited us. The music and freedom we felt together in the van carried into the rest of the day. Sometimes I spent the day off with Charlotte or Ron or someone else from the course. The Australian girl came once in a while and she usually came along with us. I don't believe I ever missed a day off in Delhi. I was always ready to get away from the course and eat.

We were dropped off at Connaught Place. New Delhi was a large city and at the Connaught Place there were restaurants, specialized shops for fabric, shoes, clothing, perfumes; just tons of shops and outdoor stalls down side streets selling anything and everything. The perfume vendors had every imaginable fragrance in tiny vials. The sweet essence of the extracts of flowers and herbs were strong and fragrant. A small drop would last all day and night. The bead vendor had all different types of beads. There were glass beads of every color. Coral was strung on long ropes and you could pick any amount of them. There were polished agates in the shape of hearts that came from Tibetan craftsmen. The fabric stalls had some of the most vibrant hues of every rich and deep color of cloth imaginable. India was a land of color. Where in Turkey everyone or mostly everyone seemed to wear black, in India, especially among the women colors were worn with boldness and beauty. Every person had some vibrancy of color adorning them. From the jewelry they wore, their clothing, down to their shoes; color, color, color. All the while the music of India was heard through the radios, always on hand at most shops or resonating in to any shop. What life. What sound and what food!

Food became an escape for me; I stored up food in my little cupboard and when fast day came around every week, I would go to my cupboard. If someone wanted to sneak off the mission to eat a *regular* meal, I was always up for it when asked. On our days off, when we went to Delhi, I would time things so that I could run and eat breakfast at a restaurant or street vendor, walk and shop, then eat lunch, then walk and browse; buy some staples for between meals at the mission. The staples would be maybe one bar of Palmolive soap and lots of food or a new skirt and lots of food; whatever I could find that was familiar or tasty. I found a shop that sold excellent white cheese -- bought it -- a market that sold lots of dried fruit where I found my favorite, dried apricots -- got some, street vendors selling freshly roasted peanuts – got 'em. I had a straw tote bag that I stuffed full and when I was done with all this shopping it would be just about time to meet up with the others to return home to the mission and perform our evening meditation.

The return drive back to the mission was usually much quieter than the outgoing one. We would discuss what we had purchased or sit quietly listening to the outside world beep and jingle its way into evening as we readied ourselves to return to evening meditation back home. Fully fed and sensory stretched, I made my way to my room, put my purchases away and put on my new purple Indian-style silk top for the evening meditation. We all gathered along the walkway; silently making our way to the temple; off came our shoes at the temple door and another day was almost over. It would be another fast day tomorrow. This is how I took a day off -- give or take a purple top or two.

And here was my routine on fast days: I would leave the temple after morning meditation. Quickly putting my sandals on, I hurried back to my room. I threw the window open and welcomed the sun light; watching the small bits of moisture on the green leaves sparkle. What fine mornings. I would take a deep breath to inhale the cool crisp morning air. Then, turning around I'd move to my little cupboard and retrieve my survival gear; peanuts and banana. I *hmmphed* and plopped onto my bed, pondered the fast, and quickly began to eat. This is how I fasted -- *not!*

"Liza, you've got to get hold of yourself!" It was Ron. He had been passing by the opened window just as I had stuffed a handful of the peanuts into my mouth. My other hand was holding the peeled banana.

I looked over at him, a little startled by his sudden appearance. I began to cry. "I know." I sobbed; chewing and talking at the same time.

He climbed into my room and sat on the bed next to me. Putting his arm around me he comforted me as I blubbered that I just couldn't help it. I had to eat and fast days made me more desperate for eating. We sat there for a while in silence as I gained control. That was pretty much how I handled the days of fasting on the mission; once a week, still meditating, no kitchen duty but lots of food selections to nibble on back at my room.

I was gaining weight and filling out. I had always been skinny so I wasn't worried about weight. As a matter of fact, the extra cushioning provided an extra buffer to the bumps in my psyche that were starting to bruise my ego.

This ravenous appetite also might have been due in fact to my not having a menstrual cycle. In my packing for the course, I didn't know how many boxes of tampons to bring but I did the math and figured I would need about seven boxes to cover me for several menstrual cycles. The compact tampons had just come on the market, so the boxes were small and easy to pack in the backpack. One thing that never came was my period. It vanished after I left Alaska and did not return until a full month after my return home.

I was concerned about this and was talking to Charlotte about it one day. What happened to my period?

Charlotte nodded. "We talked about this at Sherborne because some of the ladies there did not have periods as well. Mr. B explained that sometimes for some women, the cycle shuts down because it isn't required for the spiritual journey. In some way the body adapts or releases the energy in other ways."

Hmm, like eating everything in sight? Whatever the reason was, I did not ovulate or menstruate during the course; six months to be exact. What a break -- any woman knows what I mean on that topic.

CHAPTER 38

There were only two times that Bhante ever left our course for longer than a day. The first came on December 13, 1974. On this day we were all summoned to the temple. Bhante was sitting down waiting for us as we all gathered around him. He announced to us in a sad voice, "I am so sorry to say that Mr. Bennett has died today." He read us the telegram he had just received and held it in his hands and shook his head. He could not say much. He truly loved Mr. Bennett and his dying was an absolute tragedy to him. He would leave for Sherborne immediately to attend the funeral.

It was during this timeline as Bhante was preparing to leave for England -- we had just finished a meditation, when He turned to us and holding up two fingers said, "Sukha -- Dukha." He spoke briefly about the words -- only a small translation. Sukha was joy and Dukha was sorrow or suffering. He remained looking at us for a short while, still holding up the two fingers, he gave a slight smile, then turned and walked to his room. The tools that we would have to use on the course were dependent on how we had approached life before and what our goals were. There was no teaching by Bhante, no lectures or solutions given. In this small statement of his I believe he was communicating to us his grief (Bennett's death) and his affirmation to the process; while also defining, at least for me, the present state(s) we were working

159

through. We were on our own in one way and totally watched over in another. Unity has such a deeper meaning than the apparent lifestyle bonds we form in friendships.

The next morning a fog surrounded the mission and it seemed as though even we were pulled into the grief that was taking place in England. Those that knew Mr. B were deeply grieving by his passing. Things would never be the same and they knew it.

Bhante returned from England with gifts for all. At Sherborne there was a give-away box and all kinds of things were placed in it to share with others. Whatever was not needed by one person would be passed on to someone via the box. Bhante had gone through the box and returned with special presents for each one of us. He called each one of us into the temple and individually presented us with his gift.

When I went in, he presented me with a nice pair of black leather boots. I was amazed. The boots fit perfectly and I couldn't imagine who would give them away. I thanked Bhante. He smiled and with that sparkle in his eyes he said, "I thought you would like them." He took great pleasure in giving things. He was thrilled to see others joy. I wore those boots throughout the winter and tucked my pants into them for styling into Delhi.

Charlotte received a pair of black trainers or tennis shoes as we called them in America; new and clean. She wore them into my room and did a modeling of them, holding up her skirt and doing a model's pose. Those of us gathered in the room gave an "oooh la la" as she struck her pose.

Then came Renata …Renata was a bit of a wild card. She was extremely intelligent but where I might eat bananas and peanuts on fast days she would be meeting a beau in her room while we were all off on some project. She was popular with the locals and Bhante was aware of her lifestyle because he had known her for many years and had even performed a marriage ceremony for her.

Bhante had brought back for her a pair of three-inch spiked heels. *Where the heck did those come from -- the give-away box?* But never mind, here she came into our back room to model her sharply pointed spiked heels. They looked like an ad out of a Fredrick's of Hollywood catalog. She gave the model walk and showed off her new high heels with an added burlesque motion or two. We gave wolf whistles and I don't think I had laughed so hard in a long time. Renata took it all in fun. She was who she was and she did not pretend to be otherwise. We had a good night showing off our gifts and laughing together.

CHAPTER 39

I had just signed off on an aerogramme when Katy limped into our room. It had been a day off in Delhi for me and we talked a little about how our days had gone; she had stayed behind. She hobbled over to her bed as we visited. By this time in the course she had developed a wound on her leg. It was sore to look at and she was constantly changing bandages and dousing it with "green" oil.

As she began to remove her bandage, I looked over at her cut and cringed. She had really done a number on her leg and what a mess it was! She was in quite a bit of pain. In time her wound healed. Even though we studied the nature of disease and the mind being paramount to creating illness, it was hard to master anything to the degree necessary to ward off all the unsanitary conditions that surrounded us outside the mission walls. Infections were a concern and so were viruses that didn't affect the locals as severely as us. What might be the flu to them could be hepatitis or worse for us.

During many a meditation, I would hear rumblings come from another stall, hear the walls being moved, door opening, quickly shutting, followed by heavy running to the toilets. I empathized with that because of my struggles when I first got there. Gases like swamp fogs roamed about from time to time in the temple -- silent but deadly, and it wasn't unusual for me to know who was struggling with what by the odor that lingered in the air. We were getting to know each other far too well.

Just as we were near the end of an afternoon meditation when things were silent, a huge fart sounded out. So huge that I just knew that the person had struggled for the entire meditation to hold things back but just couldn't outwit the combustive digestion. I tried so hard not to break out in laughter for the sake of the person struggling, but a few of us started giggling uncontrollably. I was so grateful the sitting was almost over when this happened. Every level of adolescence popped up during our struggles. Bhante, of course, was not present during this particular meditation.

Like Katy, Ron was also beginning to struggle with a wound he had on his leg. He had been out late and the gates were all locked when he returned home. He had to climb over the stone wall to get inside the mission and in the process he had scraped his calf. It didn't appear to be anything but a small scratch. Then, as time went on it festered. One day I saw him struggling with his cleaning and dressing the cut just as Katy had been doing. Rags and oil, light therapy, rags and oil, more light therapy was the regime. He was tending to his wound by the colored oils table that was outside the monk's dining area. He was in pain and, ever so carefully, unwrapping his bandage.

"Let me take a look." I said

He unwound the bandage and I stared down into a blackened hole. I did a double take as I observed black skin surrounding a cavernous wound and watched his calf muscle pulsing. "Wow, I had no idea!" His pain was contagious as I looked into the quarter sized open hole. It hurt to just look at it. Ron's gash was far more severe than Katy's.

When Ron got a better, we were able to go to Delhi together and have lunch at a nice restaurant where he ordered a soda along with his meal. Soon, after we began to enjoy our meal, he began to rock back and forth complaining about his leg and its throbbing pain. He had drunk a soda before realizing that he had consumed way too much sugar and he had been warned, specifically, by Bhante, to not consume sugar while mending. "I thought I was well enough." He groaned. He was in agony the rest of the meal. I was amazed at the instantaneous "proof" his drinking of one soda had supplied to us students of the healing. It was the hard way to learn for Ron but lesson well learned for both of us.

Not long after Katy's and Ron's infections, Charlotte and Gunther became ill. This was a bad one that knocked them both off their feet and kept them in bed for many, many days. They would get up and participate or cook but their faces were hollow. So, now Charlotte and Gunther were down as well.

Aussie Paul had begun to avoid Bhante during chores. If we told him that Bhante was looking for him he would tell us to say we didn't know where he was. He was sick of carpentry work and wasn't going to hammer another nail.

During the first few weeks of the course a young French girl had arrived. She was an epileptic and had come to seek healing from Bhante's therapies. He accepted working with her and Aime, being French, was assigned the task of assisting Bhante in working with the young lady.

Aime was pulled away from us in any practical work matters. She still meditated with us and was fully on the course but she also had to attend to the French girl's color therapy and monitor her diet. I knew this was an exhaustive work for Aime. The girl was young and it was hard to get her to discipline herself from eating wrong foods and if she ate a little sugar after being on a good diet for a few days, she would go into a seizure. Once she realized that the sugar directly affected her seizures she began to watch her diet more closely but it remained a struggle for Aime to make sure the girl was being vigilant in her healing efforts.

In natural healing of any kind the person must participate in their personal therapy. It is not a "Take two aspirin and call me in the morning" practice. The therapy itself is enlightening and educating. This girl was just a teenager and she had been on years of seizure medication which had somewhat done the work for her. I have to say, I don't know if I would have done as well as she was doing for her age.

Bhante had her taken off all of the medications that had been prescribed by the medical doctors and eventually the stored up drugs began to vent from her system. She went into hallucinations and nothing would bring her back from her state of delirium. Of course this was one of the two times Bhante was away from us and out of the country.

We couldn't contact him to have him come home. I am certain I am not the only one that prayed during the meditations for Bhante to return immediately. The prayers were answered. Bhante returned within the next day and went directly to the young girl who was lying on a mattress in a guest room. He went to her and sat silently by her side for a brief time and the young lady was instantly restored to her normal state of mind. After that the young lady continued to improve but the diet remained a struggle for this young soul and her particular medical condition was one that was extremely hard to do away with.

In this time of struggles for us, Aime was kept busy to the point of exhaustion with tending to the young girl. We were all feeling the pace of the meditation and its subsequent physical symptoms.

I started talking more with the Aussie lady. She was always critical of Bhante and compared him to a famous the meditation instructor that she had meditated with before our course. At first I wasn't too keen on visiting with her. But now, in my discontent and discomfort, I was drawn to her misery.

Chapter 40

All levels began to be exposed. Humor was intense and longings for any particular meal back home were discussed to every detail. The larder was closely watched and inventoried but there was one person who took from the stash outside of the regularly planned meals. It's just what was happening to us. It wasn't the food; it was what was happening inside. Any nook or cranny of avoidance was investigated and used for full-time sensory numbing.

Chocolate, oh help me, was a main topic around the campfire. What would be our first meal back home and what kind of chocolate bar would be our first purchase once we hit the West? I had discovered Mars Bars in England and planned on making it one of my first purchases when I got there. Others mentioned Hershey bars or another chocolate confection and we went around and around about the sweet, rich flavors with roasted almonds, peanuts and/or sultanas, etc., etc.

So much so was our talking of western foods and chocolate in particular that when we heard that Adam's mom was coming to visit for Christmas we all began to talk about preparing a wish list for her to bring to us. Of course there was all kinds of excitement and laughter about what we wanted and what we would do when we got the items on our list; eat ourselves sick forget meditation,

etc. "Yeah, screw Cosmic Consciousness, I want my chocolate."
It was a long list and we expected full cooperation from Adam's
mom. I just could not wait for the day to come when she arrived,
bearing gifts.

When she arrived I waited, I think we all waited and waited.
Finally Adam came forward and sheepishly offered us what she
had brought with her. It was a paltry amount of sweets. *Can you
imagine?* I was appalled. Adam explained that once his father, saw
the list he stood firm, *absolutely not, this was just too much for us.* I
took his meager offering without any gratitude and gave him *The
Look.* I was becoming totally identified with my struggle. Adam
looked helpless and apologetic as though it were his fault, which
I, of course, let him feel it was.

Our mission animals were also acting strangely. I had heard
someone talking about Bal de Neige the rabbit being in love with
Cookie our female dog. *How ridiculous. Little Bal de Neige our
fluffy white rabbit being in love with Cookie, the dog. Who would
think such a thing?*

Well here I was now just a week later, sitting on my stoop and
watching the mission pets go about their lives. Cookie trotted
quickly by and Bal de Neige was hopping along close at her heels.
Cookie was agitated and snarled back at the rabbit but clearly
something *was* going on here. Bal de Neige was unrelenting.
When Cookie went to lie down, Bal de Neige cuddled up to her
and nibbled affectionately at her ear. It was incredible! Bal de
Neige was in love with Cookie! We had lost our sweet guinea
fowls to a predator awhile back but we still had our two ducks.
I looked over to see the rooster jumping on the ducks in an
amorous attempt at mating. *It was just too bizarre,* I thought, *just
too bizarre.* Everything seemed upside down and backwards. So

much for celibacy; it seemed the animals were acting out our most *un-celibate* thoughts!

My fellow classmate turned to me and said, "Liza, we gotta get outta here." It was as though we were peering into another world where things just didn't add up. I shook my head thinking, *and the dish ran away with the spoon.*

CHAPTER 41

As the days went to weeks and weeks to months something was happening to me. I felt darkness; as though black smoke was coming out of every pore. We had been meditating for uncountable hours when this began to happen. Duff had pointed out the intensity of the course and I really hadn't been aware of it till just then. He had listed all the meditations we were doing throughout the day and it did tally up to quite a few hours. We were definitely being effected/affected by the pace of the course.

Life was murky and all things lost their flavor. The course was descending into darker, unfamiliar territories as I became withdrawn; bothered by everything. The Aussie girl had become my compatriot and of course could we grouse.

During these times the routine continued; we still had to cook and interact with one another. One time after a few of us had just finished cooking lunch, we got into a silly little fight. It was really me and my attitude; I didn't think we should ring the bell for lunch just yet and from that I began to raise my voice arguing about the bell and when it should be rung. I was standing my ground about plates and utensils and their telling me I was being cross, and I was responding with questioning them on what we would eat off of. It was a fuss over nothing but these nothings began to poke at me. I got angry and agitated by almost anything inconvenient and I thought everything was inconvenient.

I had behaved foolishly and went and apologized. They waved it away and we continued working on the lunch meal. Lunch was served, it was great. I went and got the plates and spoons and life went on.

A good friend of Bhante's, also a monk, was visiting that day and I recall them watching us from their table that was just beyond the pit we were cooking at. The visiting monk was laughing; I am certain they understood our struggles and were glad they had moved beyond this level.

With all the boundaries coming down and layers peeling away no one seemed spared. Poor Sadhu, he just came along at the wrong time. He came with his wife in an RV with several tiny white, yipping dogs. Vu and his family were back from their traveling and had returned to the mission just a few days earlier. The young man from the RV wore his hair in a bun on top of his head and had the usual faraway look of a spiritual know it all. That look of airiness and the; *I've had a high colonic, have you* superiority. Of course he wore white and of course his voice was ever so soft. Hence, I assigned him the name of Sadhu…

One night as we were sitting around out front, Sadhu came to sit with us. He proceeded to talk about autointoxication and diet and all the other things that went along the line of food faddist rhetoric. I was boiling inside and made some emotional and inarticulate comments. But when he said that it was too late for Bhante; that Bhante was too full of autointoxication, I got really hot and started to stand up to fire away. I realized that although I had something to say, I tripped over my emotions far too often and this was no exception. I had to remain silent while the others listened intently to his talking. I left a short while later bristling inside.

Many of us would get chased by the Sadhu's dogs as we went to the well and they were getting on our nerves and it was a bad time for anything remotely agitating to occur at the mission. When it was addressed about the dogs, the Sadhu passed it off with some peace, love and light language and told us to just shoo them away with a small stick.

One morning, we heard a commotion going on in front of the temple. We had just finished morning breakfast so there was a good gathering of us when we heard words being exchanged. The arguing soon went to yelling and the next thing we saw was Vu carrying a huge long fat tree limb. Vu was not a large person but there he was cradling this huge limb, which extended outward from both arms a good foot or two. He was leaning back a little and although I don't think he was bow-legged he had a funny gait to his walking for added strength in carrying his heavy load.

"You say a stick, well here's my stick!" Vu was headed towards the dogs. He was ready to pounce on those dogs and shoo them away. Then Sadhu became red and angry, pressing into Vu's zone, there were angry words being spoken and it looked like fisticuffs any minute. Bhante was on the veranda when this all started and he quickly raised his voice to put a stop to the fighting.

Once Bhante got their attention, Vu threw down the log and walked away, but he was still hot over the dogs. They had nipped at his wife as she was taking the baby to the well that morning.

Once quiet, we all turned away from the goings on and looked at each other with amusement. No one was hurt and we never *really* expected it to become too violent but to see the Sadhu losing his cool was just too much. We all knew by then that Enlightenment wasn't that easy and right now it wasn't all that great either. I couldn't help but feel a little prideful in the Sadhu's fall from grace.

Shortly after the fight I was on the veranda with Charlotte and right in front of me Bhante was humorously speaking with Sadhu about his stance of "peace, love and light"; something to the effect of "What do you say now, my good fellow?"

"Well, I had a chapatti this morning for breakfast!" Sadhu huffed and waved his hand as his chapatti defense dialogue spilled out. *Not the devil made me do it; the chapatti made me do it?*

"Oh, paleeeeease! I can't believe it, a cha*patti*?!"

Oh, yes, there I was responding; ready to laugh out loud and say something like; *how's that for autointoxication or, oh, help me I'm being held captive by a demon chapatti spirit.*

Charlotte tugged me back and said "Now Liza, be quiet".

I looked at her and shook my head laughingly in Sadhu's direction and shut up. She was right, I had no business getting involved and karma had taken care of the rest. I got back to what I should have been doing and life went on.

The Sadhu, his wife and little nippers left within the next day or so to places unknown. We were more than slightly amused at the turmoil; watching the holy man and Vu get down and dirty. Vu's actions pretty much represented our own thoughts. It was the talk of the mission for a few days and we frankly all had a good laugh and patted Vu on the back. Vu, compassionate Vu carrying the *stick* and the young Sadhu ready for battle. It was just another crazy event in a crazy period of the course.

CHAPTER 42

Then one day, *The Log* rolled into the courtyard...

I don't know how to start talking about The Log. It was a tree that had died and fallen down on the property a season or two earlier. Bhante had the tree brought to the walkway in front of the guest quarters and it was to be used for cooking instead of using the outdoor ovens out back of the mission. It was a huge trunk of about six feet in length and four feet in diameter. To me, it was the size of a city block. We drew up a fire and for what seemed like an eternity The Log burned out front. We cooked on it, read around it during the four o'clock tea time and talked around it. It was just another nagging inconvenience to me. The cold chill of winter in Northern India kept me restless for warmth. I couldn't get clean enough and I couldn't get warm enough. The Log just kept on burning; I couldn't escape cauliflower and I couldn't escape The Log. Guests would come and we'd visit around that sooty, dark, smoldering tree trunk. I could look out Renata's window on any given day and see the smoldering trunk, waiting.

"Wherever you go, there you are". The course had me surrounded. Along with the illnesses and injuries, there I was feeling disconsolate and dark. I was even dreaming healing therapies. I hadn't expected *this* but I really hadn't any expectations so whatever happened, simply happened.

Aime had come to me to let me know that some of the group was wondering about me. "What is wrong with Liza?" I was unaware that I was so obvious. I wasn't talking much with anyone; it became hard to joke through a dilemma and impossible to eat my way out of the dark hole. I came back to my room and sat down on my bed and seriously tried to figure out what was wrong.

My contemplation revealed an answer almost instantly; I became aware of *the Law of Suffering* and understood that this law was influencing my present state of being. It was nonsensical; but consoling. My concern eased up a little. I could continue. I experienced a deep understanding yet, it came and went quickly. I had received an answer and just an answer meant that I was not forgotten in the wide and vast universe. I ran over to Charlotte and Gunther's and related the experience.

Charlotte was the most special person to me on the course and henceforth, in my life. With every insight gained from the struggle and darkest of moments, I would go to Charlotte and Gunther's; run right over to their sleeping quarters, plop myself down on their mattress and begin to talk about what had just happened. Charlotte would sit there listening nodding her head in the affirmative and then when I was through she would say. "Yes, it's just like Mr. Bennett said about XXX", and she would define my experience through what she recalled from Mr. Bennett's teachings.

So there we were the two of us, young and innocent, huddled around the knowledge and the experiences; she talking on about things that were foreign to me and me talking about experiences that were foreign to her. Our conversations were true alchemy. They were such a vital part of my life on the mission. I shared everything with Charlotte. She was a true loving soul-sister and I found consolation and definition in our talks. She is a constant reminder to me about how important friendships and personal commitments are. It was a head to heart connection that shaped my approach to all future learning. She was an absolute gem.

CHAPTER 43

I'm a little nervous here; it's a tough one to talk about in many ways. As I have stated before, Bhante never directly taught us. He maintained his distance or would just walk about smiling. There were talks during the meditation and stories of the Buddha but he never interfered with our own process of self-revelation. I didn't understand this at the time and then again many times I felt relieved that no one was seeing what I was seeing about myself. It was privately painful as I looked through the mirror darkly. I was eating a lot and boy did I continue to complain about Bhante. At first this was only an internal rub but slowly the undisciplined thought began to manifest. Nothing could be hidden forever from the Master...

"Liza, Liza!" Gambhiro called out to me. "I had a dream last night. We were talking about a celebration and you gave money to Bhante for a party and he took the money and kept it. So whatever you do, don't give Bhante the money. Don't give Bhante the money."

"Right; got it, don't give Bhante the money," I laughed and thanked him and we went on our way for the day. Well as fate would have it, not more than a day after Gambhiro's warning, the discussion of a celebration, perhaps Christmas, of some kind was brought up.

"And how will we pay for this, where is the money?" Bhante asked.

"I have some extra money; I will give some money for the party." Yes, once again, that was I popping up without thought to the prophetic dream.

"Oh so you will give us some money? Well and good... Then go get us some money." demanded Bhante.

Gambhiro looked at me horrified and was trying to wave and nod me away from getting the money.

I ignored Gambhiro, went to my room and retrieved the money and brought it outside. Bhante extended his hand and I, like a robot handed him the money. Well, that was the end of that. Not even a thank you and the discussion of how we could have the celebration continued as though the money I gave never happened.

We had no money for the celebration and I was out X amount of dollars or rupees. Afterward Gambhiro came over to me and said, "I told you not to give him the money!"

I just looked off and away. I couldn't even ponder what had happened. I had been humiliated. I didn't understand the lesson but I certainly knew I should have listened to Gambhiro; or was it just what was meant to be? Nothing mattered; karma, fate or otherwise, I had lost the razz-ma-tazz forward motion necessary to feel anything except awful to just about everything.

Chores, cooking, cleaning, meditating, meditating, meditating – the course continued.

CHAPTER 44

I looked out the small window of the Aussie girl and Renata's room. Outside, some of the group had gathered around that awful log. Did it ever end, that tree burnt forever! It was a cold morning and the sky was overcast; there they all sat looking like statues made of stone; sitting around that wretched log. Several of us were in the room, which meant several of us were not out by the log attending the discussion. I didn't care by then. I was cold and sick and tired of everything. I wrapped my shawl around me as I pulled away from the window. "I am not going out there." I turned and moved away from the window.

There I was spending more time with the Aussie girl and boy, could she pontificate. She did know a lot about India and traditions and if you remember she mentioned the possible opening of my solar plexus chakra -- even though it probably was the horrid loaf of brown sugar, which, of course, she told me was probably doused with DDT from America since it was banned in America, we shipped it over to India, etc., etc., etc.. There was no end to it. I, along with a few others, was intentionally missing meetings by this time as well. I was still meditating but refused to sit around the log.

I spoke poorly of Bhante and made sure to avoid meeting him along any of the given paths at the mission. Things came to a head when Bhante asked the young lady why she had missed a meeting. They had encountered each other in the kitchen and although I wasn't there she came back to her room and began to tell us what had happened. She was sitting on her bed looking pleased with herself with an, "I told him, didn't I?" expression on her face. If how she looked conveyed the gist of their conversation, it was confrontational. She related that she had told him things, like the course is lousy and you aren't doing anything about it. Bhante then told her if she was not happy with the situation, it was best she leave. She told him that was fine with her – *bye, bye* and by the way, not only did she feel this way but several others felt the same way also. *Gulp*.

Her biggest complaint was that Bhante did not talk about things and comparatively her famous meditation instructor was, of course, much better and encouraging. This course was beneath her; things like that, she went on about. Like I said earlier, I was pretty much grousing with her; being in such a state of denial that I was drawn to her condescending dialogue like a moth to the flame. I did, however, feel a little anxious as I listened to her; I could feel my head getting hot and red. What had I done?

Shortly after her confrontation with Bhante in the kitchen, Gambhiro came to everyone and announced that Bhante wished to have a meeting with us- immediately. We all gathered around the log. Bhante sat up on the porch area above us; the Aussie girl and the British man that had come with her were absent; they were both leaving. Bhante went on to explain what had happened between the young lady and him and repeated what the young lady had told him about us; what we had been saying about him. He now humbly asked to know what he had done to offend us and what was our response to her statement?

I spoke up and said a few things. He replied to me and I then brought up the money he had taken from me. I talked a little while and I can't remember if anyone else said anything. I had spoken up to him and making it clear that I was confused about him and what this was all about. I felt detached as I spoke; at this point in the course, which was right after the New Year, I was numb and suffering deeply. The nothingness hung around me with considerable torment, and even denying Bhante could not produce a flicker of conscience. There was such a struggle within me; one that knew what I was doing was wrong but also didn't have a clue as to *what* was wrong.

The meeting ended and I was removed as kitchen steward and without formally announcing it, I was shunned by Bhante. I was allowed to be on the course but I was nothing to him -- absolutely nothing.

A few days later, after the meeting around the log, Gambhiro and Duff held a meeting with some of us in the back yard and asked us what the matter was, encouraging us to think about what we were doing. I remember being cynical and thinking to myself, *what a joke, Duff asking **us** to get it together.* As I recall, none of us responded to their talk with us; I know I didn't. The meeting ended and we went our separate ways. Again that struggle within; divided and pulled; feeling guilty and smirking at the same time.

I went and visited with the Aussie girl as she packed up to leave; part of me was relieved she was going. It was a cowardly relief, but I knew she didn't belong there. Then again where did I belong? That nagged at me. And Bhante continued to say nothing. He didn't reply back to anything I had said that day around the log. He carried on with equanimity -- there was a hint of displeasure -- maybe.

"Sherborne is heaven compared to this." I was told by a former Sherborne student. I sat visiting some time and then went back to my room to sit and reflect. No amount of complaining settled a deeper nagging. What was happening? I just couldn't figure it out or get a handle on it but something, an intangible something, was tapping on my door and peeking through the keyhole. *If only for one day I could leave here and just rest and let nothing enter my mind. Just one day was all I would need.* I had been designing my fantasy suite at a five-star hotel for some time now. In my mind I would go to the hotel, get a room and stay for just one night and a whole day. I would have a hot bath and call home to Alaska. Then, I would have room service bring me trays of hot western foods and eat as much food as I could. The room was imagined to every detail and it became an escape for me.

Apart from my fantasy, I reflected like crazy. As much as I hated to face it I began to observe a pattern of my personal life was being exposed. It was painful to think of but was there something to this idea of a pattern?

In the quiet of my room, I self-reflected. It was difficult to come to terms with what I was seeing. I had to admit that I was seeing a pattern in me that kept recurring. I pondered the course and reaffirmed my commitment to seek training– I had come to learn and be taught; accepting that I knew India was where I should be, and that Bhante was in charge; that I was meant to learn from Bhante.

Even though I could not understand what was right or wrong, I had to admit that according to my affirmation of the course, etc., Bhante was right and I had to be wrong. "What is it in me that keeps repeating this?" I searched deep. "Please, help me to understand, help me to see what it is in me that keeps causing this cycle" I prayed. It was an uncomfortable, humbling moment for me and I kept driving home the observation of repeated actions. I truly felt terrible about everything, but it was no good to feel terrible; it was important for me to find some sort of solution to the recurring nightmare I now found myself in. I felt helpless and lost as I reviewed events and humbled myself in contemplation and prayer.

That little bit of humility and honest soul searching received an answer. Slowly a shaft of light began to trickle into my mind's eye and in that shaft of light I saw before me what I can only describe as fleshy, beige colored tuber with many roots. The bulb was long; shaped like a sweet potato. As the light expanded, I peered into its many small roots and was taken inside these pathways which looped out, around, and back to the tuber. Each root was an event that had occurred in my life; going back to my earliest childhood; long forgotten but retained and "living" inside. Not only was I able to view events from memory but I also traveled, if you will, back in time *into* the events; not just hearing words spoken, emotions felt; but viewing and experiencing each individual action almost simultaneously. Rather than shrinking away in horror, I sat and let the illuminating moments be self-revealed. The tuber was functioning as the junction box that controlled every action by creating a "first response". And in this moment, *I got it! I had met the enemy and she was me! I was struggling with myself.*

I was aware that the struggling and suffering for all of the weeks and months was brought about by an unconscious effort to sabotage my freedom. In letting go of clinging to old ways and habits or blaming someone else, I literally heard a cracking sound as though a huge nut had been broken open and I was literally inside the dimensions of my own existence.

This was also a defining moment for me in the perspective from which I had always viewed living; from the inside out. It took years for me to understand this more fully but from this moment on I was a witness to my own life.

As usual, I ran to Charlotte's and Gunther's anxious to talk about what had just happened. Charlotte listened carefully as

I recounted my story. Once I finished talking she related my experience to a topic discussed in work groups; the topic of a *chief feature*, which by all accounts appeared to be what I saw as the junction box. As I said before, it was difficult to comprehend how some of the actions were connected but in retrospect, I came to see that when I experienced the actions separately; one after another, it was not the connection between actions but rather the actions attachment to the chief feature. Incredible as it may sound I was seeing and experiencing the cause of my struggles.

Imagine there is a barrier that keeps you from entering your home. In one room is your head and in another room is your heart. They are both part of the place you dwell but until the blockade is leveled you don't really have a clue on how to fully live within your home. This barrier is our ignorance. Even if one is born self-aware one still needs a defining moment. Mystic and Intellectual alike must struggle with "seeing" in such a way so that a discipline is established and true Work begins.

It took Bhante's steadfast silence and energy; in order that we might fully experience for ourselves our personal Work. He was willing to sacrifice everything on our behalf even if it meant losing some of us. During the hardest of times on the course he said nothing. He would smile; sometimes distance himself, but he held firmly to the value of the personal experience. Once again -- *The proof was in the pudding.* We were never meant to rote his teachings. Bhante liberated us from the need to depend on anyone but ourselves.

"Do not be afraid to see the ugliness that is within you. It is better to see these things and know this ugliness; that way you will become free from its influence."

Bhante's statement might seem a little harsh but from the perspective of one knowing oneself, it is a truism that helps the mirror darkly become the bright window of self-consciousness.

Choices either make us Serious Seekers or side-line critics. Try as you may, you can't be both for long.

What an amazing few days I spent basking in the peeling away of layers and the lifting of heaviness; to feel the shafts of light trickle into my veins and arteries. The discontent vanished and I was on an incredible high.

CHAPTER 45

It was probably not more than two weeks or so after my *Enlightenment* that we were told that Bhante had actually consented to allow us to leave the mission for an overnight stay in Delhi. It was Independence Day and celebrations would be taking place all over India. Maha Vera, a monk that was close to Bhante, had invited all of us to stay at his flat in Delhi and enjoy the celebration. There was to be a parade that would be close to the apartment where he and his sisters lived. Bhante's acceptance of this generous offer meant no evening meditation-followed by no morning meditation! It was somewhat surreal to think we had over a day away from all of our structured activities. *First Enlightenment; now this, what?* We all talked about it and as many of us that could were planning to go. By the end of the week (or whenever it was; it could have been in the middle of the week for all I know.) we headed out of the mission for Maha Vera's.

When we arrived at Maha Vera and his sister's, we ate a small meal they had prepared for us and visited with them for a short while. They were friendly and I felt grateful for their kindness and hospitality. After this we all piled into the van and Duff took us to a local disco. I had never been to a discotheque before; it had a huge dance floor surrounded by tables and chairs. The lights were dimmed and in all it was a comfortable setting. The crowd of people there seemed to consist of Westerners and young Indian men. All the current music was being played so it was exciting to hear what seemed endless familiar tunes and not have to go home to meditate. We selected a couple of small tables to set our gear down and then went out on the dance floor and danced the night away. What a time, we had all resolved our struggles; our health was on the mend so it was a true celebration; we were releasing all kinds of pent up energy. Our small group was the last dancing when Duff told us it was time to leave.

Together, we all headed across the dance floor to the exit. Just when Ron and I were on the dance floor and the others had exited, John Lennon's *Imagine* came over the sound system. I looked at Ron and said, "We gotta dance to this!" And as the soft and gentle piano introduced Lennon's lyrics, Ron and I began our last dance together. John Lennon and his song *Imagine* in particular said it all; what I envisioned as a new world and the hope of peace -- yes, what I imagined. Ron and I quietly sang along with John Lennon; as we moved slowly across the floor. When the song ended we ran out the door to the waiting van. Ron took a place and sat down right across from me in the back of the Mercedes van. I smiled and looked at him as we drove through the streets of Delhi -- wild and free.

"India, 1975"…

"Oh mom, not again" my children are telling me.

"We're at a Discotheque in Delhi. It's time to leave; we've been dancing for hours and are heading for the door when *Imagine* comes on. Ron and I look at each other…"

My children can tell the story better than I can these days. It is a memory that remains brilliant and alive. Every time *Imagine* comes on, they look at me with a not again -- please tell us again look.

"Please, always imagine a better world." I tell them. "At least imagine it. Imagination counts"

We made our way to Old Delhi; the honest to goodness real Delhi where authentic Indian culture was still awake and active in the streets; even at this late hour. Old Delhi is the original city -- before the British built New Delhi -- there was just Delhi. We went into an old café and Duff ordered a traditional yet exquisite sweet dish. It consisted of clear noodles drenched in heavy cream that was perfectly sweetened with white sugar. It was stunningly good and yet so simple. There were fewer noodles than cream which made it light and tasty to where the noodles and the liquid did not compete or overpower each other. Oh, Yummmmmm!

As I sat in the café in Old Delhi, I gazed outward to the Indian people and breathed in the smells of their rich culture; shaking my head with regret that I had not gotten to Old Delhi before this. I had grown fond of Indian life and felt more at home with the traditional Indian lifestyle than I did with the tourist haunts of New Delhi. The outdoor clippety-clopping of the horses, jingling of bells and the occasional quacking of horns from the scooters speeding by as we supped on the authentic Indian dessert; our faces animated and bright from the dancing frenzy, gave me such Joy. Love poured out of me as I watched Indian life pass by. India was now home to me and more than that, India would always be the place where my True Life began.

We made it back to Maha Vera's. He was still awake and was enthused to see that we had all had such a good time. We found places to lie down and were each given a blanket. We laughed a little as we said our good-nights, tucking ourselves into our individual wooly cocoons. The next morning they prepared a breakfast for us and after this we took to the streets to find a place to watch the parade. The streets were packed but we had managed to get there early enough.

The parade was festive with all the usual bells and whistles and military displays of power. There was even a military unit that wore tiger skins over their uniforms. I had never seen anything like it before. I was told they were the elite forces that were fierce warriors. I was impressed at their display of brute force.

Parade over; it was time to return to the mission. We got back and spread out to our various quarters, telling those that stayed behind at the mission about the great time we had all had. It was later in the afternoon when we got home and as the day went to night just after the meditation, the usual shutting of doors and muffled good-nights and plans to go to the chai shop could be heard on the pathway. Tromp, tromp; sounds slowly fading away as some made their way to the hostel for chai and talk. I stayed behind in my room reading *The Hobbit*.

Apology Accepted

The time came one evening during the meditation, after we were all settled and the silence prevailed over our every thought, that Bhante addressed us. "It is taught that above all things; one should always obey the Teacher because it is the Teacher that will show you the way to be free from this world. If you have wronged the Teacher in any way, then you must apologize. If you cannot apologize to your Teacher face to face, then you must do so in your meditation."

We then went into our evening meditation. I got the hint and boy, did I apologize to Bhante in that meditation! I went over my revelations and how I had come to understand what I had done, leaving no detail out. I also wanted to be sure that I shared everything with him so that there would be no barrier between us. His approval or acknowledgment of the experience was vital to me. I was so grateful that he knew how to allow dialogue or meditation on this because I had no idea on how to approach him; to humble myself in apology and explanation. I did so in that evening meditation. My apology was sincere and heartfelt.

As we left the temple that night, I quietly whispered to my friend, asking her if she had apologized. "Like crazy" was her answer. We looked at each other, without saying it we understood that we were grateful for the second chance.

That's how we reconciled to Bhante and from then on things were back to normal. I didn't get the kitchen back, but I had Bhante and his loving kindness was more than anything else I had wanted at that point. It was a joyful time on the course. The darkness had lifted and I was experiencing newness to life. I had the force of an idealist as I entered into the search for the Kingdom of God but had come out realizing that all the force and knowledge in the world amounted to nothing without self-awareness. *This is where it begins.* Kingdom of God 101 had ended and I had passed my finals.

Bhante and I became even closer through the experience. It was a trust thing, of course. We still didn't talk much but the understanding was there. I was plugged in to his presence that did not require heavy language or grandstanding on his part or mine. I was a devotee. He would never expect anyone to be *his* devotee; it was a devotion to the experience and the possibilities that lay within the awakened self.

"What I am, anyone can become." Bhante said this often and within that statement was the approach he took in sharing all that he ever had.

CHAPTER 46

It was early March of 1975 when the course ended. Bhante asked me to make the mission my home -- to come and go as I pleased but to always return to the monastery. I told him that I wanted to return to Alaska and although he would never force me to do anything, I could tell he was saddened. He gave me his blessings to return to the world.

What emotions swept over me; leaving friends that were now part of my life. There would not be another group like this for me and I knew it. I had gotten to know each one of them in their darkest struggles as they did mine, and although we didn't discuss much I personally recognized the suffering we had all been through. I also watched as layers of likes and dislikes and judgments were stripped away revealing each classmate as my valuable Teacher. So Duff, the one I bumped up against so much became my greatest Teacher; as respected as any other classmate.

Now the ending was near. Humbled and ready for the world; I was leaving and with the same trepidation I had in coming, I had in my leaving. The course had changed my life and I felt that only those that endured the last few months with me in India would understand or know me so well. I trusted these few people with my life.

During my private talk with Bhante he told me to let everyone know that the course was ending but did not give a date. "Just let them know that it will be ending soon." So that is what we did -- we let each other know we had completed our course. There was a thrill of happiness and excitement in the air. I was young and didn't think that it would be years before I would see my beautiful spiritual brothers and sisters again...Some, never again.

The cameras came out and pictures were taken. We exchanged addresses, giving assurances that we would write to each other, etc., etc.

Paagal came up to me during this final stage of the course and indicated to me that he had heard I was leaving. I nodded. He took the small patch of his dirty head wrap that hung down in his face, feigning tears and wiping them away. He walked away and to everyone he passed he stopped and pointed to me and made a hand gesture of wings rising to the sky. Then he took that dirty old rag and wiped imaginary tears away. He did this for the remaining days I had on the mission. We still laughed a lot but our together times always ended on the same note with his tears, rag wiping and wings to heaven gesture.

"Liza, you've got to see this! I went to town and had the film developed. Look at the picture of Paagal!" It was Ron who was coming up to me on the path. I stopped and leaned in to look at the pictures he was holding.

I remembered the day Ron had taken this particular picture he was showing to me. We had all been popping off pictures of each other and things in general and Paagal would not be ignored. He came to Ron and yanked at Ron's shirt; insisting he be photographed right then and there. Paagal stood to attention with his beat up old rake held proudly to his side and looked straight into the lens; picture taken.

Now here was Ron back from town with his pictures and handing me the picture of Paagal. "I can't believe it. What happened?" I asked Ron.

"I don't know; all the other ones turned out."

He was correct, all the other photos were clear and showed us all in various hi and good-bye type poses. Paagal's picture however showed no person in the picture.

"Look at that smudge, it looks like smoke." I told Ron. There in the photo was a plume or mist. Paagal was nowhere to be seen.

We looked at each other, puzzled and then laughed. Who else but Paagal could pull a trick on us like that? I always felt he did it on purpose -- let us know something about him. I didn't need a botched picture to tell me that Paagal was something much more than he ever let us know. He had certainly become something much more to me. He was on the course with us; he knew us and still took the time to be a friend.

CHAPTER 47

It was still dark when I got up and dressed. I cannot remember who drove me to the airport, but Bhante and my closest friends, came along to say good-bye. The drive to the airport was quiet to the point of somber. I was anxious to get on with life but oh how I hated leaving my beloved friends, beloved family. I took my place in the queue and as my turn came to present my ticket and baggage, I took one last look at the group -- turning back to wave. To this day I can still see Charlotte in her vintage fur coat, she and Gunther drawn tightly together. Bhante's face was grim. Ron looked around not knowing how to react. My heart was aching and I began to cry.

The inspector smiling kindly said to me, "And when will you be returning to India?" I turned and took my place in line and slowly boarded the jet.

Far below me was the same land and countries we had driven through. We were up so high that I couldn't distinguish where one country began and the other ended. Between clouds passing by I searched as hard as I could to spot something familiar below but of course it was impossible. How I longed to see the Khyber Pass just one more time.

We passed over France at sunset and the Eiffel Tower rose tall in the sky as France seemed rounded to the horizon. I didn't notice anything accept the Eiffel Tower which made me think of the old Disney movies I had watched as a child on world travel; there's a colorful map of Europe and Donald Duck is wearing a beret and pointing to Paris. I mean it was just so clear.

Finally, there was England! Amazing how distinct the land was here in Europe. Of course we were descending by this time and the land became more defined. No sooner did Europe appear than to disappear into the sunset; turning into night as we began a final descent into Heathrow Airport.

I looked out the window of the jet to the lights of London; watching the traffic going to and fro. *Whoosh!* The energy hit me like a blast of hot air. I realized that I had been completely sheltered for months. Below me was the hustle and bustle of one big city. In India I had lived a secluded Life; yet life with a capital L. Here in the "real world", life; with a small l, was brilliant and dazzling, eclipsing the big L. India was miles away now as though the massive hands of God had folded it into the past. The memory would be the leavening for my future but for now as I looked out the plane window all I could see were the bright lights of London.

As I disembarked I talked with other passengers and was told to go to the Victoria Station area for a bed and breakfast. I took a bus from the airport directly to Victoria Station and walked down one of the streets looking for a B&B and performing my *left/right* walking meditation. It was late by now and the streets were empty and quiet. It had been raining and the streetlights reflected in pools on the black pavement.

Several long blocks later I spotted a bright yellow Victorian building with a black awning. It was the Elizabeth Hotel. How appropriate, I thought. I rang the buzzer and was let in. I took a room on the second floor.

The room was small with just a twin sized bed in the corner under the only window in the room. I had a sink in my room, one chair and a small night stand. The rest of the toilette facilities were down the hall. I was so excited to be spending the night in an honest to goodness B&B that the romance of communal bathrooms and toilettes only added to my expectations of cheaper accommodations and world travel. It was a comfortable room small enough to feel safe with no unnecessary frills.

I took my first bath in many, many months at the Elizabeth B&B in London, England; in the spring of 1975. *AHHHH!* I soaked for as long as I could. Unlimited hot water! It seemed a whole layer of skin was peeled away and floating in the tub. I had bathed regularly at the mission and never felt dirty but as I looked at the water I realized I hadn't had a good soak for about five months or more. I quickly dried and returned to my room. I hopped into bed just too tired to think and fell quickly to sleep.

CHAPTER 48

The next morning I looked out the small window of my room and saw the backs of many of the same Victorian-era style buildings. The roofs were black and tiled and the buildings were not as brightly colored as the facades in the front street area. I tried to see if there was anyone at any other window but I didn't see a soul. Curtains covered most of the windows and each building had a backdoor leading out to a small community courtyard. I spotted a small kitchen table across the way in one window. There was a pretty cloth on it with a small vase of flowers placed in the center. I stared expectantly; waiting to see activity. Alas, no life was visible. I was alone.

After dressing I went down the stairs to the basement level for my breakfast. The basement was a half basement with windows looking out to the streets. It was a nice size and there were tables of all shapes and sizes covered with clean tablecloths and seating was random. I chose a table close to one of the windows so that I could watch the street scene of people and cars passing by. Another couple came and sat with me and we struck up a conversation. They were traveling to Amsterdam, recently married, etc. A pot of coffee was placed on the table and I was given a choice of ham, bacon or sausage with eggs and toast. Once again I drank endless cups of coffee with cream and sugar and spread the jam thickly on the heavy wheat toast. I ate bacon that day and the eggs were scrambled. It was a perfect place to land after the seclusion of India. Life was good but oh, how I missed India.

After eating, I set out for Piccadilly. I had jet lag and culture shock so stepping out amongst the living in London felt like sleepwalking. The faces, the gestures, all things were as though I were watching a movie. No one noticed but it took me a few minutes to gather myself up and become a tourist or something western again.

The stores displayed their wares but it was all boxed up now, such a change from the stalls of India. I even missed the DDT soaked loaves of brown sugar. It was an overcast day with no rain expected so that I could walk and browse the windows with ease. I did a little shopping then went to get something to eat.

For starters, I purchased my much fantasized about Mars bar. The first bite I took disappointed me. I held the wrapper out to view and wondered if this was the candy bar that I had eaten in London prior to India. I knew it was a Mars bar but the flavor was all wrong now. It didn't satisfy any urges and I discovered that I was eating it as a token for the days, nights, weeks and months I thought/dreamt and fantasized about chocolate. What distraction one candy bar had provided!

When I returned to the hostel, I began to plan the last part of my travel. I would take a train to Botley to deliver messages and remedies from Bhante to the Myat Shi's, then on to Sherborne to deliver letters from friends and family left behind in India.

The next morning I made it to the train station, purchased my ticket, walked around for a bit, and then boarded my train. The seating was booth-type; two benches that flanked an old wooden table. I took an empty booth, sat down, and began to write Bhante. I had picked out a card in Piccadilly; blank inside with little purple flowers drawn on the front.

As the train pulled out of the station, I glanced out my window, admiring the beauty of England. Turning back to my writing I concentrated on what to write Bhante, which was difficult; somehow *having a good time, wish you were here* wasn't what I wanted to say.

Sometime during my writing, I received a direct mental impression "put down your writing and look up", which I did. Across the table from me sat an elderly gentleman. I wasn't aware of him before this. I nodded and said, "Hello".

He nodded back to me. At this point came a small rustling of energy moving down the aisle. It was a young lady who quickly sat down next to the elderly gentleman. She was hurrying along because, as she huffed and puffed her explanation to us, she was running late and had almost missed the train.

The elderly gentleman had already begun a conversation with me, which quickly became a three-way talk. I didn't question the inner prompting I had received; it seemed quite natural at the time. He asked me questions and I replied. Where was I coming from? *India, I have just completed a course of study, etc...* What had I learned and how would I use it? *I had discovered myself and was certain that I needed to return to the world at large and expose my newly awakened state to as many circumstances and cultures as possible -- By living in the world the possibilities for self-growth and observation were endless. This would allow me to understand life and its diverse nature through the window of self. Rather than college, my university would be humanity.* I went on to say that I knew that all knowledge came from the degree of knowing oneself and to grow, I needed exposure. I had fully accepted the responsibility of "Working on myself". He listened and nodded from time to time. I also expressed a need to be in the world to affect change -- not just in me but change in others as well. We were all connected and I wanted my connection to contribute to others Self-Awakening.

The young lady had just completed a stint in the Royal Navy and was on her way home to marry her fiancé. She was an avid sci-fi reader (_Dune?_) and she related to many aspects of our conversation through her reading of sci-fi material. I was amazed that sci-fi held such depth; I have never liked science fiction. As the conversation wound round our personal futures it became increasingly clear that, for me, going back to Alaska and the world at large was the right thing to do. I became more settled in my leaving the mission and began to look forward to getting back to Alaska.

The length of the trip was spent talking with one another along the lines I have described. This elderly gent showed an air of calm reserve and as we talked I took a little longer look at him as I answered his questions. Not so much as to stare, I knew that would be obvious, but who was this man that had prompted my attention without one word being spoken?

The first thing I noticed was his skin which was like a newborn baby's; fresh and youthful. The skin also had a radiant quality to it so that although it resembled the soft, unblemished skin of youth it was even more than that; there was a soft pinkish glow to it. His eyes were a clear blue, straight ahead -- forward – penetrating, but not intimidating. He looked directly at me when he asked questions. I felt comfortable with his questions and as I answered his questions, I became clearer in my thoughts about my future. In retrospect, I would say that I was being interviewed. His hair was pure white, silken, shiny. He had a refined nose that was long and narrow. What I also noticed was the faint outline of two small veins that stood out on his forehead. One was about center of the forehead and went up to the scalp area and the other went over and up to his scalp. He wore a beautiful angora or mohair neck scarf which was knit in horizontal stripes of purple and brown. While looking at this beautiful scarf I felt he held a deep sentimental attachment to it. Perhaps it had been made by his loved ones? If there is one thing I wish to emphasize, it is the almost common nature of our visit. Anyone looking at us would have seen three people carrying on a normal conversation.

He was the first to leave our group. As he stood and moved past me I turned and looked up at him.

"See you later," I said in an almost too self-assured manner.

He looked at me; squarely in the eyes and slowly nodded in the affirmative. It was a, "You can count on it" look.

When he left the train I turned to Sue and said, "That was a special man."

She affirmed that and we continued our conversation as the train pulled out of the station. I got off at the station nearest the Myat Shi's and took a cab to the gate house.

CHAPTER 49

I spent the night at the Myat Shi's. We had a good visit and Mrs. Myat Shi was excited to hear all about Bhante and the course. We talked for some time, then I went to my quarters; the same one that I had slept in before we left for India. Memories flooded over me as I thought of Ron's playing the recorder so many months earlier. I took to the bed and dozed off. I arose early to catch another train to Sherborne to deliver the letters. I had said my good-bye to Mrs. Myat Shi the night before so I quietly closed up quarters and walked down the long driveway to the highway below. It was just dawn as I headed out hitching a ride to the nearest train station.

I took the train as far as I could and hitch-hiked the rest of the way to Sherborne. I hadn't called ahead to let anyone know that I was coming so when I arrived and entered the school, I asked the first person I met where I might go to find Pierre to deliver the letters. I was pointed in the direction of the Faculty Room.

After knocking lightly on the door to the room, I entered. No one was there at the time. There was a table with chairs but what caught my eye was a photograph on the far wall. I went closer to look at it. It was hung a little higher than most pictures so I had to look up and into the picture. I instantly recognized the figure in the photo as the man on the train. The two veins on his forehead were visible, yet I still wondered to myself; *could it be the elderly gentleman?* I was looking at a man that displayed none of the radiant qualities of the gentleman on the train yet it was he; there was no mistaking it. I just stared in silence pondering the mystery of it all. It was Mr. Bennett and he had died December 13th of the previous year...

Epilogue

I returned to Alaska and married my boyfriend, Jake. India was more than a memory. It settled in deeply and with uncanny dispassion revealed the process of my human experience. Connected to the heart with its every beat and percolating throughout my body in the rushing of blood, the awakened state went on and on until more experiences of a deeper nature put me on or lead me up to even loftier heights: Unimaginable and life changing.

Bhante has been gone for over ten years. I think of him every day and of course there are those dreams I have when I spend a little time with him. I miss him but I also know that I will see him again. What a colossal experience it was for all of us that sought out the **Opportunity for Serious Seekers** course of a lifetime.

We were all so young to have been given so much. That highly concentrated dose way back when would take years to unfold and expand through the dilution of human relationships and life in general but what an incredible journey; and how grateful I am for the love Bhante gave to me back in 1974.

May all beings be well and happy.

Made in the USA
Middletown, DE
05 July 2022